Table of Contents

Foreword

Before you is the second edition of the *Canadian Reference Guide to the United Nations*. Compared with the original 1994 publication, this new edition has been considerably enriched in terms of both the content as well as the more vibrant, diversified visual presentation.

The 1999 Guide contains a wealth of new information, particularly on Web sites of the UN and of all its specialized agencies, institutions, commissions, committees and other related organizations.

The Guide is meant to be a practical reference tool, one that is easy to consult and simple and enjoyable to use. It is not a work for specialists. Instead, the Guide is aimed at students, teachers, the general public, the news media and all who seek to know more about this great institution.

The United Nations system is as vast as it is complex. It touches all spheres of human activity and affects people throughout the world. The *Canadian Reference Guide to the United Nations* shows how important is the role played by the UN in our daily lives. The Web addresses found in these pages will enable those wishing to learn more about the UN system to increase their knowledge and better appreciate this institution, which is so central to Canada's foreign policy.

Enjoy the read, and good luck in your research!

Communications Bureau
Department of Foreign Affairs and
International Trade
Ottawa, Ontario K1A 0G2, Canada
www.dfait-maeci.gc.ca

UN/DPI photo

i

Message from the
Prime Minister

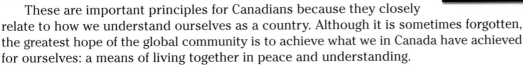

For over 50 years, the United Nations has embodied Canada's highest hopes for a world at peace. There are simple reasons for our commitment to the UN: it stands for the rule of law, social and political justice, international co-operation and the setting of universal standards, as well as the peaceful resolution of disputes.

These are important principles for Canadians because they closely relate to how we understand ourselves as a country. Although it is sometimes forgotten, the greatest hope of the global community is to achieve what we in Canada have achieved for ourselves: a means of living together in peace and understanding.

The United Nations has struggled against racism and colonialism, against disease and illiteracy. It has stood up for those who have no voice—the oppressed, including millions of women and children around the world.

The UN has contained many conflicts and brought relief to their victims. But the work is far from finished: peace remains elusive for millions around the world, the gap between rich and poor countries is far too wide, and the rights of nations and of individuals under international law must still be defended.

The United Nations and its family of specialized agencies have established a framework for multilateral relationships among states—for disparate activities ranging from co-ordinating the distribution of mail and the registration of patents, to co-operation in the management of the world's oceans and outer space. They have also set and defended universal norms and values, co-ordinated research and technology transfers, and promoted sustainable development in many fields.

While there may not be an immediate solution to every problem, we value the means by which we can pursue potential answers together with mutual respect, tolerance, accommodation and compromise.

Today as much as ever, we need the United Nations to maintain international stability and order, and to tackle issues that know no borders.

Canada's strong commitment to the UN and its humanitarian principles is a reflection of our deep, unyielding belief in the future—a belief helping us build a country that the United Nations has named the best country in the world in which to live.

Jean Chrétien

Jean Chrétien

Message from the Minister of
Foreign Affairs

Since the United Nations came into being in 1945, Canada's commitment to it has been unwavering. After 54 years, and in an increasingly globalized world, the UN still provides the best hope for co-ordinated and integrated solutions to the major issues facing the planet at the beginning of a new millennium.

New threats and challenges—terrorism, crime, drugs—arise from a world in which the face of conflict has changed. Economic and social insecurity is mounting worldwide, and increasingly the well-being of the individual is at risk. As a result, a new security concern—human security—is emerging as a global issue.

We must work together to confront these challenges, and this means working through a vibrant United Nations. A key factor in Canada's decision to run yet again for a seat on the United Nations Security Council was our recognition of the UN's central place in a global system. Canada was successful in its bid and began serving a two-year term on the Council on January 1, 1999. In electing us to this seat, the UN membership was acknowledging Canada's long-standing contribution to promoting peace and security around the world.

We have made human security and the protection of civilians in armed conflict the cornerstone of our agenda for our term on the Security Council. But well before beginning our Council term, Canada was working to advance human security in other ways. Our leadership in the international efforts to ban anti-personnel mines is a clear example. Although the Ottawa Convention banning such mines was not negotiated through UN channels, it now resides with the UN and is enshrined as part of the UN legal system. Only the UN has the capacity to give the Convention the global weight it needs to be an effective international safeguard.

Canada also led in another recent global effort to protect human security. From our preparatory work to chairing the negotiating conference, Canada strove vigorously to establish the International Criminal Court—an international tribunal mandated to try cases of crimes against humanity, genocide and war crimes.

These recent actions are representative of Canada's long-term commitment to the United Nations and to the UN's central role as the most important multilateral body in the world.

Producing the *Canadian Reference Guide to the United Nations* is a modest way of helping Canadians, and others throughout the world, understand that role by explaining the key functions of the UN and its many components, agencies and commissions. It is also a way to highlight the importance of the UN to Canada, plus Canada's part in the history and effectiveness of the UN as a vital global institution. I hope you will find it an informative and useful tool.

Lloyd Axworthy

Preamble to the Charter of the United Nations

We the people of the United Nations determined

to save succeeding generations from the scourge of war, which twice in our lifetime has brought untold sorrow to mankind, and

to re-affirm faith in fundamental human rights, in the dignity and worth of the human person, in the equal rights of men and women and of nations large and small, and

to establish conditions under which justice and respect for the obligations arising from treaties and other sources of international law can be maintained, and

to promote social progress and better standards of life in larger freedom,

And for these ends

to practise tolerance and live together in peace with one another as good neighbours, and

to unite our strength to maintain international peace and security, and

to ensure, by the acceptance of principles and the institution of methods, that armed force shall not be used, save in the common interest, and

to employ international machinery for the promotion of the economic and social advancement of all peoples,

Have resolved to combine our efforts to accomplish these aims

Accordingly, our respective Governments, through representatives assembled in the city of San Francisco, who have exhibited their full powers found to be in good and due form, have agreed to the present Charter of the United Nations and do hereby establish an international organization to be known as the United Nations.

Overview of the
United Nations

UN photo 165054: Lois Connor

Overview of the United Nations

Introduction

The United Nations officially came into being on October 24, 1945. By that date a majority of the 50 countries that had signed the UN Charter in San Francisco on June 26, 1945, had ratified it in their national parliaments. The UN replaced the League of Nations, which had been created by the Treaty of Versailles in 1919. Canada, a participant at the San Francisco Conference (April 25 to June 26, 1945), is one of the founding members of the United Nations.

The actions of the UN are guided by its Charter, which defines the United Nations' purposes as follows:

- to maintain international peace and security;

- to develop friendly relations among nations; and

- to achieve international co-operation in solving international problems of an economic, social, cultural or humanitarian character, and in promoting and encouraging respect for human rights.

The actions of the United Nations are based on certain principles:

- all of its members are equal;

- all members must fulfil their Charter obligations;

- international disputes are to be settled by peaceful means;

- members may not use force or the threat of force against other members;

- members must help the United Nations in any action it might take in accordance with the Charter; and

- the United Nations may not interfere in the domestic affairs of any state.

Currently, there are 188 member states. For a complete list of member states, along with the year each was admitted to the UN, see Section 10 of this Guide.

The UN resembles a world parliament, although it does not legislate in the manner of a national parliament. But through their actions and their votes, its members help set international policy.

The United Nations family

The United Nations family has six main organs: the General Assembly, the Security Council, the Economic and Social Council, the Trusteeship Council, the International Court of Justice, and the Secretariat. All act in concert with dozens of related specialized agencies, funds and programs in order to develop an increasingly co-ordinated but diversified action plan in the spheres of peace and security, humanitarian assistance, human rights, and economic and social development.

The United Nations family also includes 16 organizations, each operating in its own particular field of expertise (e.g., health, funding, agriculture, civil aviation, telecommunications). These specialized agencies, such as the World Health Organization, the International Civil Aviation Organization and the World Bank, along with the six main UN organs, make up what is called the United Nations system. A brief description of the roles and functions of these 16 organizations can be found in Section 9 of the guide.

General Assembly

All member states have seats in the General Assembly. The Assembly can discuss all matters within the scope of the UN Charter. Its recommendations carry moral weight as an expression of world opinion; however, the General Assembly cannot compel action by any nation. Decisions on important questions—peace and security, admission or expulsion of members, budgetary matters—need a two-thirds majority. For other issues, only a simple majority is required.

The regular session of the General Assembly begins each year in mid-September and continues until mid-December. Special or emergency sessions are sometimes convened when circumstances warrant. When the Assembly is not in session, its business is conducted within special organs and committees.

The General Assembly receives reports from all other UN organs, appoints the Secretary-General and members of other UN bodies, approves the budget, and directs the work of the Secretariat.

The General Assembly has six main committees:

- Disarmament and Related International Security Questions (First Committee);

- Economic and Financial (Second Committee);

- Social, Humanitarian and Cultural (Third Committee);

- Special Political and Decolonization (Fourth Committee);

UN/DPI photo: Milton Grant

- Administrative and Budgetary (Fifth Committee); and

- Legal (Sixth Committee).

Security Council

The Security Council is the main organ responsible for maintaining global peace and security. It has 5 permanent members —namely, China, France, Russia (which assumed the Soviet Union's seat), the United Kingdom and the United States— and 10 members elected by the General Assembly to serve two-year terms. On October 8, 1998, Canada was elected to serve a new two-year term as a non-permanent member; this is the sixth time since 1948 that Canada has sat on the Security Council. The new term runs from January 1, 1999, to December 31, 2000.

Council members are on call 24 hours a day in case an international crisis occurs. Any UN member or the Secretary-General may call a Security Council meeting if a threat to peace exists. Even a non-member state may request a meeting if it feels that such a threat exists. When a meeting is called, those countries directly involved in the issue under consideration are invited to take part in discussions but they may not vote on Council resolutions. It takes a nine-member majority for a resolution to be carried, but none (except for procedural questions) can be adopted if opposed by one of the five permanent members (giving them a "veto").

In the event of a conflict pitting one or more countries against another, the Council can order economic sanctions against the aggressor, and all other UN members are obliged to comply with these. If the sanctions fail to stop the aggression, the Security Council can authorize member states to launch joint military action, as it did in the case of the Korean War in 1950 and when Iraq invaded Kuwait in 1990, as well as in Somalia, Rwanda and Haiti. Although these operations were approved by the Council, they were conducted entirely under the authority of the states that launched them. The Council authorizes such operations only as a last resort, when all peaceful means of resolving a dispute have failed.

In most cases, the Council tries to negotiate a cease-fire between the combatants. Once the fighting stops, UN peacekeeping forces may be sent to keep the two sides apart or to help implement a peace accord.

Last, the Security Council recommends the admission of new members to the UN. It also makes recommendations on filling the posts of Secretary-General and of judges on the International Court of Justice.

UN/DPI photo: Milton Grant

Economic and Social Council

The Economic and Social Council (ECOSOC) is the real backbone of the United Nations system. Under the authority of the General Assembly, the Council is the principal co-ordinating body for the economic and social activities carried out by the UN and the various funds, programs, organizations and specialized agencies that make up what is called the United Nations system or extended family. It has 54 member states, each elected for a three-year term. Canada's last term on the Council ended December 31, 1998.

The activities overseen by ECOSOC are aimed at promoting economic growth and progress in the developing world, respect for human rights, and international co-operation in such areas as housing, family planning, environmental protection and crime prevention. More specifically, ECOSOC's main functions and powers are as follows:

- to serve as the main body for examining international economic and social issues of a global or interdisciplinary nature and for developing, on the basis of studies and reports commissioned by the Council, practical recommendations on these issues for member states in the economic, social, cultural, education, public health and other related spheres;

- to ensure effective, universal observance of human rights and basic freedoms;

- to convene international conferences on questions in its areas of expertise and prepare draft conventions for submission to the General Assembly;

- to co-ordinate the activities of specialized agencies while consulting with them and making recommendations to them, as well as to the General Assembly and UN member states; and

- to consult the over 1500 non-governmental organizations (NGOs) enjoying consultative status with the Council on questions that come under its scope.

To successfully carry out its mandate, the Council has several commissions and committees with specific responsibilities. This structure includes nine functional commissions charged with studying issues and making recommendations in their fields of expertise. They are as follows:

- the Commission on Human Rights;

- the Commission on Population and Development;

- the Commission for Social Development;

- the Commission on the Status of Women;

- the Commission on Crime Prevention and Criminal Justice;

- the Commission on Narcotic Drugs;

- the Commission on Science and Technology for Development;

- the Commission on Sustainable Development; and

- the Statistical Commission.

The Council also has regional economic commissions charged with promoting economic development in each region, and strengthening economic relations among the various countries there and between these countries and the rest of the world. They are as follows:

- the Economic Commission for Africa (Addis Ababa, Ethiopia);

- the Economic and Social Commission for Asia and the Pacific (Bangkok, Thailand);

- the Economic and Social Commission for Western Asia (Beirut, Lebanon);

- the Economic Commission for Europe (Geneva, Switzerland); and

- the Economic Commission for Latin America and the Caribbean (Santiago, Chile).

The Council also has four standing committees: (1) the Committee for Programming and Co-ordination; (2) the Commission on Human Settlements; (3) the Committee on Non-Governmental Organizations; and (4) the Committee on Negotiations with Intergovernmental Agencies.

Last, the Council supervises the work of a great many expert bodies on questions such as the environment, natural resources, and economic, cultural and social rights. It also oversees the governing boards of several UN organs, including the United Nations Children's Fund, the Office of the High Commissioner for Refugees, the World Food Programme and the United Nations Population Fund, to name but a few.

Trusteeship Council

The Trusteeship Council is the only UN body that is no longer active; however, its mechanisms are still in place and could be re-activated if circumstances change. It was originally set up to ensure that the governments charged with administering the territories under UN trusteeship (11 at the time of the Council's inception) suitably prepared them for autonomy or independence. Its role came to an end in 1994, when the last of these territories —Palau, an island group in the Pacific Ocean, which had been administered by the United States—opted for a new status. The Trusteeship Council, which had been composed of the five permanent members of the Security Council, will not sit again unless required by special circumstances.

International Court of Justice

The International Court of Justice (also called the World Court) is the United Nations' main legal organ. The Court sits in The Hague in the Netherlands and has 15 judges, who are elected by the General

Assembly on the recommendation of the Security Council. In selecting judges, care is taken that the principal legal systems of the world are represented. The Court settles legal disputes between member states and renders advisory opinions for the UN and its agencies. Only member states may refer issues to the Court. A state can refuse to submit to its jurisdiction (except where otherwise expressly provided by treaty), but if it accepts, it is obliged to comply with the decision rendered.

Secretariat

The Secretariat is headed by the Secretary-General and provides the services that keep the UN and the programs of its five main bodies running on a day-to-day basis (those organs being the General Assembly, the Security Council, the Economic and Social Council, the Trusteeship Council, and the International Court of Justice). The Secretariat operates out of UN headquarters in New York, as well as offices in Geneva, Nairobi and Vienna.

The Secretariat employs about 8600 civil servants—4700 of them in New York—from 170 countries. Their duties include administering peacekeeping operations, organizing international conferences, studying world economic and social trends, preparing studies on such subjects as human rights, disarmament and development, providing simultaneous interpretation and translation services, and providing information on the United Nations to media the world over.

Budget and personnel

The UN budget for the year 1999 is US$1.25 billion. This amount covers the operations of the Secretariat for the United Nations system in New York, Geneva, Nairobi and Vienna, as well as the five regional economic commissions. In addition, there is the UN funds and programmes budget, which comes to nearly US$5 billion for the year 1999. Added to this are the budgets of specialized agencies such as the World Bank and the International Monetary Fund, bringing total operating expenditures for the entire United Nations system to over US$18 billion a year.

The Secretariat and the various components of the United Nations system are funded through member states' dues and through donations from the private sector, other national and multilateral agencies, and individuals. Member states' dues are set according to total gross domestic product (GDP), adjusted for a series of factors including per capita income and population. For the year 1999, Canada's share was set at 2.754 percent (US$28.6 million).

Including Secretariat staff, UN personnel total slightly over 52 000 people working in 29 agencies, institutions and programs of the UN system throughout the world.

Main Spheres of Activity of the United Nations

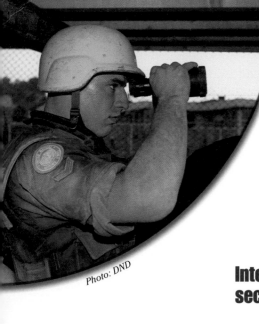
Photo: DND

Main Spheres of Activity of the United Nations

International peace and security

Along with economic and social development and the protection of human rights, international peace and security—whether their achievement or their preservation—have always been and still remain the central concern of the United Nations and the international community.

Through the Security Council, whose main responsibility this is, the UN has helped settle disputes between nations, prevent conflicts and put an end to fighting. It has conducted complex peacemaking and humanitarian operations, and has played a crucial role in resolving some of the longest-running conflicts of recent years.

To carry out this mission, the UN uses various means ranging from unobtrusive diplomatic initiatives undertaken during unofficial meetings to the deployment of military contingents, often called Blue Berets, made available by member states.

Maintaining international peace and security is a collective effort that requires the active involvement of individuals, countries and organizations. The UN Secretary-General plays a major role in peacekeeping and in restoring peace in

the event of armed conflict. He acts both personally and through his special representatives. He can call the Security Council's attention to any situation that might jeopardize international peace and security, can lend his good offices in mediation or can take discreet diplomatic initiatives. He also practises preventive diplomacy to avert the outbreak of hostilities.

International peace and security are also a priority for an increasing number of countries working together to create innovative coalitions and partnerships in order to further global action on human security issues. For example, with Norway's support, Canada has established a flexible framework for promoting co-operation between countries with common views from all continents, with the aim of achieving progress on issues that affect human security, such as children in armed conflicts and small arms proliferation.

In addition, broad coalitions of non-governmental organizations and states co-operate with the United Nations to promote peace in the world, along with protection of human rights. The very rapid passage of the Convention on Anti-Personnel Mines (the Ottawa Convention) may be the finest example of this new collective approach in favour of international peace and security.

Last, multilateral organizations, such as the Commonwealth, La Francophonie, the Organization of American States, and the Organization for Security and Co-operation in Europe, are working, sometimes independently and sometimes in conjunction with the UN, to prevent new conflicts or end ongoing ones.

Peacekeeping

The most visible and spectacular type of UN action is still the deployment of peacekeeping missions. Since 1948, the UN has conducted about 40 peacekeeping operations, 30 of them within the past 12 years. Taking part in these have been over 750 000 military personnel, 1500 of whom gave their lives for the cause of peace.

Thousands of police officers and civilians have also served in these operations. It was in recognition of their contribution to world peace that the Blue Berets received the 1988 Nobel Peace Prize. In the minds of many people, the best symbols of the United Nations are the UN peacekeeping contingents at work in the four corners of the world.

In the beginning, in the late 1940s, the first United Nations peace soldiers were unarmed military observers posted along cease-fire lines in Kashmir and the Middle East. It was not until 1956 that organized units were deployed during the Suez Crisis: Lester B. Pearson, then Canada's Secretary of State for External Affairs, suggested using peace soldiers to separate the belligerents after they had agreed to a cease-fire. This operation has been used as a model for almost all peacekeeping missions launched by the United Nations since that time. Mr. Pearson himself received the Nobel Peace Prize in 1957 for this contribution to world peace.

In recent years, UN peacekeeping missions have become much more complex. To traditional and essentially military tasks, such as supervising cease-fires, separating belligerents and maintaining buffer zones, have been added political and humanitarian activities. Civilian police officers, election observers, human rights observers and other civilians have joined the UN peace soldiers. Their duties include ensuring that food aid gets through, and helping former adversaries implement complex peace agreements.

Working with the United Nations agencies and other humanitarian organizations, the Blue Berets have helped refugees return to their countries, monitored respect for human rights, and undertaken mine clearance and reconstruction work. UN peace soldiers have also been used for disarming and demobilizing former combatants, training and supervising civilian police, and organizing and observing elections.

Every peacekeeping operation is sent in by the Security Council, which rules on the size of the operation as well as its general objectives and timetable. Since the UN does not have its own military forces, member states decide whether to participate in a mission and,

CIDA photo: Roger LeMoyne

11

*To receive regularly updated information on ongoing peace-keeping operations, visit the UN Web site at **www.un.org** and click on "peace and security."*

if so, they determine what type of personnel and equipment they are prepared to offer.

To succeed, a peacekeeping mission needs to meet certain conditions. In particular, it must have a clear and feasible mandate, effective command, political and financial support from the UN member states and, above all, co-operation from the parties to the conflict. The mission has to be undertaken with the consent of the government of the country where it is deployed and, generally, of the other parties involved; and in no case must it be used to promote the interests of one party to the detriment of the other.

Impartiality is the primary "weapon" of the peace soldiers, who in any case carry only light arms and cannot use force except in cases of legitimate self-defence or when armed persons attempt to prevent them from carrying out their assigned duties.

Last, peacekeeping by the UN must not be confused with peace enforcement or other forms of military intervention. On many occasions, the Security Council has authorized member states to use "all necessary means," including force, to end armed conflicts or threats to peace. With this authorization, member states formed military coalitions in 1950 during the Korean War and in the 1990s in response to the invasion of Kuwait by Iraq, as well as in Somalia, Rwanda, Haiti, and Bosnia and Herzegovina. Although sanctioned by the Security Council, such interventions are entirely the responsibility of participating states.

Peacebuilding

The term "peacebuilding" first gained currency in 1992 with its appearance in the landmark report entitled *An Agenda for Peace*, by Boutros Boutros-Ghali, then UN Secretary-General. This document outlined the new challenges and opportunities for promoting international peace and security in the post–cold war world.

One of the principal challenges for the United Nations has been the proliferation of conflicts within states. In 1997, for example, of the 87 armed conflicts around the world, 84 of them were within states. Nearly all these conflicts took place in developing countries, and they have often been characterized by long-term cycles of violence. While conflicts generally occur within states rather than between them, they tend to spill over into surrounding areas, with dire consequences. Growing international awareness of the human and financial costs of such conflicts has prompted the UN and the international community to think differently about international security, and has led to the emergence of the concept of peacebuilding.

Peacebuilding is the effort to strengthen the prospects for internal peace and decrease the likelihood of violent conflicts. Its goal is to enhance the indigenous capacity of a society to manage conflict without violence.

Peacebuilding lies at the intersection of international security and development. It may encompass a wide range of activities. For example, support for conflict prevention and dispute resolution, demobilization

CIDA photo: Roger LeMoyne

of combatants, resettlement of displaced persons, local institution-building, election monitoring, democratic and judicial reform, civilian police training, and post-conflict economic and social reconstruction are all activities with important peacebuilding dimensions.

As the linchpin of the global security system, the UN has a critical role to play in all these areas. Many activities related to peacebuilding are in fact carried out by modern peacekeeping operations, as these have expanded their scope to deal with new realities. However, peacebuilding is a wider concept than peacekeeping because it seeks to deal with the root causes of conflict, to address not only the immediate but also the medium- and longer-term challenges for ensuring peace in troubled areas.

Active in peacebuilding at the UN are not only the Security Council and the office of the Secretary-General, but also other specialized agencies, including the United Nations Development Programme (UNDP), the UN High Commissioner for Human Rights (UNHCHR), the United Nations Children's Fund (UNICEF), the UN High Commissioner for Refugees (UNHCR) and the United Nations Civilian Police. Regional organizations (e.g., the Organization for Security and Co-operation in Europe, NATO, the Organization of American States and the Organization of African Unity) as well as a range of national and international non-governmental organizations are working with the UN on these challenges. Finally, through its two-year term on the Security Council, as well as through national efforts such as the

Canadian Peacebuilding Initiative, Canada is striving to enhance the capacity of the UN to undertake effective peacebuilding activities in areas of conflict.

Disarmament

Stopping the arms race and reducing, and then completely abolishing, the arsenals of weapons are main UN concerns. The UN has commissioned research and made recommendations. As a permanent forum for dialogue, it has facilitated negotiations conducted at the bilateral level or within the Disarmament Conference meeting regularly in Geneva.

In 1996, the General Assembly crossed a historic watershed when it passed the Comprehensive Nuclear-Test-Ban Treaty (CTBT), which banned all nuclear testing. The previous year had seen a great step forward, when the states parties to the 1970 Treaty on the Non-Proliferation of Nuclear Weapons (NPT), ratified by 187 countries (all but 4 members of the international community), extended its provisions indefinitely. Under this treaty, states possessing nuclear arms promised not to supply them to other countries and to reduce their own nuclear arsenals. Countries without nuclear arms undertook not to acquire such weapons.

The concern with disarmament has been unwavering over the last 30 years. During this time, the UN has presided over the conclusion of treaties banning the emplacement of nuclear arms in space (1967), or on the seabed and the ocean floor (1971). Other treaties banned the development,

*For more information about the Canadian Peacebuilding Initiative, visit the Department of Foreign Affairs and International Trade Web site at **www.dfait-maeci.gc.ca** or the Canadian International Development Agency site at **www.acdi-cida.gc.ca**.*

CIDA photo: Brian Atkinson

production and stockpiling of bacterio-logical (1972) and chemical weapons (1992), limited conventional armed forces in Europe (1990), and banned or limited the use of certain types of weapons.

The International Atomic Energy Agency, based in Vienna, is responsible for enforcing the guarantee agreements reached under the various disarmament treaties in order to ensure that nuclear materials and equipment intended for peaceful uses are not diverted for military purposes.

Canada has always been closely involved in these issues and in the nego-tiation of multilateral disarmament treaties. On all these matters, Canada's position on non-proliferation, arms control and disarmament has been based primarily on maintaining, defending and strength-ening the application of three basic global treaties: the Treaty on the Non-Proliferation of Nuclear Weapons, the Chemical Weapons Convention, and the Biological and Toxin Weapons Convention. These basic instruments are comple-mented by the Comprehensive Nuclear-Test-Ban Treaty and the treaties creating Nuclear Weapon-Free Zones.

Also in connection with nuclear dis-armament, Canada is encouraging the United States and Russia to speed up the process of implementing the Strategic Arms Reduction Talks (START) agree-ments reached between these two countries. Although Canada is pleased that implementation of START I, which came into force on December 5, 1994,

seems to be ahead of the agreed timetable, it is still concerned at Russia's delay in ratifying the START II treaty signed on January 3, 1993. Finally, to reassure states in all areas of the world about their own security and to achieve some progress on various other security issues debated at the United Nations and in other forums, Canada is calling for a rapid start on negotiating a START III treaty, which it regards as essential to the pursuit of nuclear disarmament.

Anti-personnel mines

Under Canada's leadership and the collective efforts of a broad coalition of states and non-governmental organizations from all over the world, substantial progress has been made over the last two years on the issue of banning anti-personnel mines, culminating with the signature in Ottawa on December 3 and 4, 1997, of the Convention on the Prohibition of the Use, Stockpiling, Production and Transfer of Anti-Personnel Mines and on Their Destruction. The Ottawa Convention, signed by 135 coun-tries and already ratified by over 84 states, assumed the force of international law on March 1, 1999.

Under the provisions of the Con-vention, states signatory undertook in particular to: *(a)* provide data on their stocks of anti-personnel mines and their national implementation measures to eliminate these mines; *(b)* destroy all their stockpiled anti-personnel mines within 4 years following passage of the convention; *(c)* destroy the anti-personnel mines in minefields within 10 years; and

CIDA photo: Brian Atkinson

(d) co-operate with Convention enforcement measures.

The UN estimates that tens of millions of such mines are buried in over 70 countries, and that a further 2 million are still being set every year. These devices, often undetected, kill or mutilate some 20 000 people a year. It is estimated that by the end of 1998, even before the Convention had officially come into force, over 11 million mines stockpiled in 15 countries had been destroyed and a new global norm against their use had virtually ended the international trade in these deadly weapons.

Canada is in the forefront of the international drive to get rid of these mines: in December 1997 it created the Canadian Landmine Fund, with a budget of $100 million over five years. This amount will be used to help several countries conduct mine clearance activities, to provide assistance to victims, to develop new mine-detection and mine-destruction technologies, and to help signatory states comply with the treaty. So far, Canada has made a $10 million contribution for mine clearance and assistance to victims in Bosnia and Herzegovina, and another contribution of almost $3 million for similar programs in seven countries in Central Europe, Africa and the Middle East. Last, nearly $4 million has been committed for mine clearance and support to community rehabilitation programs in Central America.

Economic and social development

Together with international peace and security, economic and social development forms the most important component of the UN's work in the world. The United Nations believes that there cannot be lasting global peace until all peoples experience well-being. The UN Charter states clearly that the United Nations' principal functions must include promoting higher living standards, full employment, and economic and social progress. The United Nations therefore delivers numerous programs to improve living conditions throughout the world, and commits a very large part of its human and financial resources to these activities.

Three quarters of the world's people are concentrated in developing countries, and it is estimated that 1.5 billion of them are living in poverty. The per capita average annual income in the world's 49 poorest countries amounts to US$360, whereas it is more than US$23 000 in the richest 24 countries, or 65 times greater. As the gap is growing, one of the priorities and essential tasks of today is to close it.

To try to do this, the UN has a number of tools, one of which is to hold world conferences that focus on major problems and attempt to identify practical solutions. Over the past 10 years, the UN has organized world conferences on the environment and development (1992), human rights (1993), the correlations between population and development (1994), social development (1995), improving the status of women (1995), human settlements (1996), and food security (1996).

CIDA photo: Roger LeMoyne

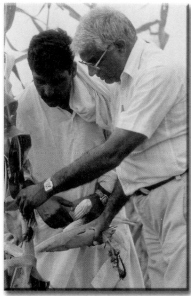
CIDA photo: Roger LeMoyne

Every 10 years since 1961, it has also adopted International Development Strategies recommending measures to reduce the gap between the poor and rich countries.

But it is mainly through agencies and specialized programs that the UN works to achieve its mission in the economic and social fields. The United Nations Development Programme is the spearhead of this effort. This is the program that funds most UN development activities, operating in 174 countries and territories, with an annual budget in the order of more than US$1 billion. In addition, the activities it supports generate added annual investments of over US$9 billion from donor countries, specialized agencies, NGOs and the private sector.

The United Nations Children's Fund works with children so that they are protected and can live in conditions allowing them to flourish. With an annual budget of nearly US$1 billion, UNICEF is active in 150 countries; its programs deal with such needs as vaccination, health care, nutrition and basic education.

Many other UN agencies are working on development in conjunction with governments and NGOs. For example, the United Nations Environment Programme (UNEP) promotes preservation of the natural environment and measures to combat pollution throughout the world. The World Food Programme (WFP) is the main international food aid provider.

In the area of population, when developing countries need assistance they go

first to the United Nations Population Fund (UNPF). As for the United Nations Centre for Human Settlements or UNCHS (Habitat), it works to improve housing conditions for some 600 million people living in unhealthy surroundings.

Last, the United Nations Conference on Trade and Development (UNCTAD) promotes international trade, especially by seeking to increase the integration of developing countries into the world economy. Section 8 of this Guide provides a detailed description of the mandates, objectives and activities of these agencies and programs.

In addition, 16 specialized UN institutions, connected with the United Nations by special agreements, develop standards and directives, help draft policies, and provide technical and other forms of practical assistance in virtually all areas of economic, social and developmental life. These institutions include the World Bank (IBRD), the Food and Agriculture Organization (FAO), the United Nations Educational, Scientific and Cultural Organization (UNESCO), and the World Health Organization (WHO). These institutions and their activities are described in Section 9 of this Guide.

Canada is a very active participant in all the major United Nations programs, commissions and committees, and in the activities of specialized UN agencies and institutions, in part through its development assistance program managed by the Canadian International Development Agency (CIDA). The Agency contributes about $150 million a year to the core budgets of the various UN agencies dealing with the many facets of development. This participation in the UN organs is important to Canada, enabling it to take part in development efforts in many more countries and sectors than it could have done with only its own bilateral development assistance program.

Whether in programs addressing basic needs—family planning, nutrition, education—or programs dealing with health, environmental protection, women's education, agricultural development, food, irrigation, the eradication of poverty, the protection of human rights, humanitarian aid or vaccination, Canada is present wherever its resources permit and where its action may serve to improve the lot of the world's poorest people. It participates not only through CIDA but also through a number of federal departments, including Agriculture and Agri-Food, Environment, Transport, Natural Resources, and Justice, to name but a few.

Human rights

Since its founding in 1945, the UN has attempted to achieve the objectives of justice and equality defined by the Charter and applying to individuals as well as to states. One of its first tasks was to draft the Universal Declaration of Human Rights (see p. 62 of the Guide), which enshrines the basic rights and freedoms that all human beings can claim: the right to life, liberty and nationality; freedom of opinion, conscience and religion; the right to work; the right to education; the right to take part in the nation's public business, etc.

The Declaration, the first draft of which was written by a Canadian, John Peters Humphrey, was passed a little over 50 years ago by the UN General Assembly on December 10, 1948. Every year, Human Rights Day commemorates this event, which is unique and of fundamental importance in the history of humanity.

Two international agreements adopted in 1966—the United Nations Convention on Economic, Social and Cultural Rights, and the United Nations Convention on Civil and Political Rights—extend the area of rights established by the Declaration. These three instruments together make up the International Charter of Human Rights, both a standard and a goal for all nations and all peoples.

Since that time, they have been joined by about 60 other instruments concerning human rights, notably the International Convention on the Elimination of All Forms of Racial Discrimination, the Convention on the Elimination of All Forms of Discrimination against Women, the Convention against Torture, and the Convention on the Rights of the Child.

To afford better protection for human rights and ensure that they are respected, the UN has acquired certain tools. The United Nations High Commissioner for Human Rights, a position created in 1993, co-ordinates all the activities of UN system agencies in this area, attempts to prevent violations of basic rights, investigates violations

CIDA photo: Roger LeMoyne

that do occur and works with governments to remedy such problems.

The UNHCHR also serves as Co-ordinator for the International Decade of the World's Indigenous People (1995–2004), which was proclaimed by the UN General Assembly to highlight the importance of improving the situation of Indigenous peoples worldwide. A major objective of the International Decade is adoption of a declaration on the rights of Indigenous peoples. Another UN initiative is the Working Group on Indigenous Populations, created by the Commission on Human Rights in 1982 to promote and protect the human rights and fundamental freedoms of Indigenous peoples; this meets annually in Geneva.

The Commission on Human Rights is the only body that, when breaches of basic rights are brought to its attention, examines them in public sessions. Through its Special Rapporteurs, the Commission also studies the situation in all member states and monitors more closely the conditions in certain of them.

CIDA photo: Stephanie Colvey

Canada has played a leading role in the development and adoption of most of these conventions and instruments. Indeed, the protection and promotion of human rights has long been a basic and integral component of Canadian foreign policy. Canada feels that multilateral bodies, such as the United Nations, are often the most effective instruments for influencing governments and advancing the cause of respect for human rights in the world.

When very serious violations occur, the UN has special tools at its disposal. For example, in 1993 the Security Council created an international tribunal to try persons accused of committing war crimes during the conflict in the former Yugoslavia. A similar tribunal was set up for Rwanda in 1994. Up to September 1999, a Canadian, Louise Arbour, was the chief prosecutor of both courts.

With substantial Canadian leadership, global efforts are under way to implement the newly established International Criminal Court, which will provide a permanent tribunal for prosecuting cases of genocide, crimes against humanity and other war crimes.

Humanitarian affairs

When a country is struck by war, famine or natural disaster, the UN and the agencies that belong to the UN system furnish assistance to the population. Under the United Nations Emergency Relief Co-ordinator, who directs the UN's Humanitarian Affairs Department, organizations such as the World Food Programme, the United Nations Food and Agriculture Organization, the United Nations Children's Fund, the United Nations Development Programme, the World Health Organization and the United Nations High Commissioner for Refugees work together and deliver part of this assistance directly.

In recent years, for example, the UN and the agencies of the extended UN family have assisted tens of millions of people who were victims of conflicts or natural disasters in the former Yugoslavia, the Great Lakes region of Africa, and various regions of Asia and Latin America.

As a member of the Security Council since January 1999, Canada has made the protection of civilians in armed conflict a priority. Under our Council presidency in February, a special debate was held on this topic.

Canada's annual contribution to the different humanitarian aid programs in the UN system varies depending on the the conflicts and natural disasters of the day. On average, however, this contribution may range from $200 to $300 million per year. It is channelled mainly through UNDP, WFP, UNICEF, the UNHCR, and the United Nations Relief and Works Agency for Palestine Refugees in the Near East (UNRWA).

Canada's Department of National Defence (DND) is also often called upon in natural disasters or within the framework of UN peacekeeping missions. Canadian military aircraft transport emergency relief, and Canadian troops often distribute the aid directly to disaster or conflict victims. Canadian soldiers particularly distinguished themselves in this respect in the conflict in the former Yugoslavia, bringing in provisions and medical supplies often at the risk of their lives.

International law

The United Nations has greatly contributed to extending the primacy of law by codifying and developing international law. The UN has been behind hundreds

of treaties and conventions dealing with virtually all realms of human activity, from international trade to environmental protection, and including international terrorism, civil aviation and telecommunications. It has given particular attention to protecting basic rights.

Among the most important of these instruments, the number of which is now approaching 500, are the Convention on the Elimination of All Forms of Discrimination against Women (which enunciates the principle of equality of the sexes), the United Nations Convention against Illicit Traffic in Narcotic Drugs and Psychotropic Substances (an essential tool in the struggle against the drug trade), and the United Nations Convention on the Law of the Sea. This last has been called the most complex of all legal texts developed by the UN to this day; it aims to ensure access to the riches of the sea for all countries under equitable conditions, to preserve the marine environment from pollution, to promote freedom of navigation and to facilitate research.

Canada has been and continues to be highly active in the area of codifying law at the international level. For example, the Law of the Sea Convention, which entered into force in November 1994, in particular bears a marked Canadian influence. It was actually Canada that convinced the rest of the international community that the oceans are part of the common heritage of humanity and should therefore be protected.

CIDA photo: Roger LeMoyne

Canada and the
United Nations

CIDA photo: Peter Bennett

Canada and the United Nations

The United Nations is the only multilateral organization whose membership approaches universality and whose agenda encompasses all areas of human activity, in every region of the world. It is, in effect, the marketplace at which much of the world's multilateral diplomacy is conducted, and the mechanism through which the views of the international community are given expression.

It is also the forum in which grievances are aired and, with member state consensus, resolved. The UN's ability to live up to its founders' ideals, and to its potential, is almost exclusively determined by the 188 countries that collectively constitute the United Nations. Our successes are its successes; our failures, its failures. This organization can only accomplish what its member states allow it to.

Canada has been an active and committed participant in the United Nations since its founding in 1945 in San Francisco, where Canada took a leading part in the drafting of the UN Charter. Individual Canadians have played vital roles within the United Nations, and many of the UN's great accomplishments have had a Canadian dimension. For example, John Peters Humphrey was the principal author of the Universal Declaration of Human Rights 50 years ago; Lester B. Pearson helped invent the concept of peacekeeping, winning the Nobel Peace Prize for his efforts to resolve the 1956 Suez Crisis; and Maurice Strong chaired both the 1972 United Nations Conference on the Human Environment, in Stockholm, and the 1992 United Nations Conference on Environment and Development, in Rio de Janeiro, serving as well as founding Executive Director of the United Nations Environment Programme.

Canadians have occupied key positions within the United Nations system, including the Presidency of the General Assembly (Lester B. Pearson, in 1952–53), and Canada served on the Security Council in 1948–49, 1958–59, 1967–68, 1977–78 and 1989–90. In January 1998 a Canadian, Louise Fréchette, was appointed the first-ever UN Deputy Secretary-General.

The UN's basic purposes and its other underlying principles have guided Canadian foreign and defence policy from the outset. Over the past half-century, Canada has made a significant, constructive and sustained contribution in all areas of UN activity: peace and security, development assistance, human rights, and social, economic and environmental affairs.

As the cornerstone of a rules-based international system, the UN has always been a vital forum through which we have sought to influence world affairs, to defend our security and sovereignty within a stable global framework, to promote our trade and economic interests, and to protect and project Canadian values such as fairness, equal opportunity and respect for human rights.

The promotion of human rights and justice, the prevention and abatement of environmental degradation, the alleviation of poverty, and the promotion of development and human security on a global basis —these can be achieved only through multilateral discussion and negotiation. The sole global forum available is the UN. It is therefore no surprise that support for the UN is deeply entrenched throughout Canadian society.

The UN remains as relevant to Canada today as it was in 1945, if not more so. The 1995 Foreign Policy White Paper, *Canada and the World,* put it unambiguously:

The UN continues to be the key vehicle for pursuing Canada's global security objectives. Canada can best move forward its global security priorities by working with other member states. The success of the UN is fundamental, therefore, to Canada's future security.

Canada has participated in virtually every major UN peacekeeping operation. The UN remains a vital instrument through which Canadians and others are working to bolster human security by ridding the world of anti-personnel mines, halting the traffic in military small arms or putting an end to the conscription of children as soldiers. Most recently, Canada chaired the negotiations leading to the creation of an International Criminal Court, thereby helping to end impunity for war criminals.

Canada gives particularly strong support to the ongoing process of UN reform, in order to help ensure that the organization remains responsive to the interests and concerns of its membership, and capable of dealing with threats to global security. To this end, Canada is pledged to work to strengthen the UN's capacity for preventive action, to enhance the UN's rapid reaction capability, to improve the functioning of the UN's decision-making bodies and to put the UN on a sounder financial footing.

We are the eighth-largest contributor to the UN budget, after the United States, Japan, Germany, France, the United Kingdom, Italy and Russia. Our share amounts to US$28.6 million, or 2.754 percent of the UN's budget for the year 1999. We always pay our annual assessed contributions in full, on time and without condition.

Canada is a member of all the UN specialized agencies. It takes part in all major UN programs and is actively engaged throughout the United Nations system. We have seven diplomatic missions accredited to the United Nations: in New York (Permanent Mission of Canada to the United Nations), Geneva (Permanent Mission of Canada to the Office of the United Nations at Geneva, to the Conference on Disarmament, and

CIDA photo: Peter Bennett

to the World Trade Organization), Montréal (Permanent Mission of Canada to the International Civil Aviation Organization), Nairobi (Permanent Mission of Canada to the United Nations Centre for Human Settlements and the United Nations Environment Programme), Paris (Permanent Delegation of Canada to the United Nations Educational, Scientific and Cultural Organization), Rome (Permanent Mission of Canada to the Food and Agriculture Organization) and Vienna (Permanent Mission of Canada to the International Organizations in Vienna).

Public opinion surveys consistently show that Canadians have a high regard for the UN. In fact, 90 percent of Canadians in a recent poll said that Canada should continue to put a high priority on its role in the UN. The United Nations is not perfect; indeed, as noted earlier, it is only as efficient and relevant as its 188 member states allow it to be. The UN has, however, demonstrated the ability to adapt, institutionally and operationally, as new issues have emerged and as relations between countries continue to evolve. The United Nations remains crucial to Canada and, we believe, essential to the conduct of diplomacy in an ever more interdependent world. It is a precious resource that we are committed to preserving.

CIDA photo: David Barbour

Following are some of the major sectors of UN activity in which Canada has been, and will continue to be, particularly active.

Security Council

For the sixth time since 1948, Canada has a seat as a non-permanent member of the UN Security Council. Canada's term on the Council runs from January 1, 1999, to December 31, 2000. Canada intends to make use of its term to work for progress on issues to which it attaches particular importance: promoting the concept of human security, including conflict prevention and peacebuilding; human rights; and humanitarian issues. Canada will also work to make the Council more open, transparent and responsive to all UN member states, and to make it more representative of new geopolitical realities.

Peacekeeping

Since its beginnings in 1956, peacekeeping has become an integral and high-profile component of UN operations. Since 1957, when Lester B. Pearson was awarded the Nobel Peace Prize for his leadership in developing the concept of peacekeeping, Canadians have felt a commitment to peacekeeping and have accepted frequent requests to join the Blue Berets in operations around the world.

One of a growing group of countries to which the UN regularly turns when it requires peacekeeping advice and expert military contributions, Canada has participated in almost all the peacekeeping operations mandated by the UN Security Council—in Cyprus, Bosnia, Haiti and elsewhere.

Canadians have served in more than 30 separate missions. Among them have been men and women from the Royal Canadian Mounted Police, Elections Canada, the Canadian Red Cross, and other governmental and non-governmental agencies based in Canada.

In 1994, Canada established the Lester B. Pearson Canadian International Peacekeeping Training Centre in Cornwallis, Nova Scotia. The Centre offers instruction in the theoretical foundations of peace-keeping, as well as its more practical aspects.

In 1995, at the 50th session of the UN General Assembly, Canada presented a ground-breaking study on a UN rapid reaction capability. The study urged the UN and its members to develop a rapid deployment capability, which could be swiftly mobilized to respond to humani-tarian crises. It also recommended the establishment of an operational-level headquarters for force deployment. The study's recommendations are already being acted upon by the UN.

Peacebuilding and human security

Canada's traditional role as a peace-keeper is today being complemented by our leadership in responding to two of the most significant challenges we face in the post–cold war world: peacebuilding, or building sustainable peace in countries prone to recurring cycles of violence; and human security, or promoting the safety and security of people.

Canada was one of the first countries to promote the concept of peacebuilding

CIDA photo: Brian Atkinson

in 1996, when it launched the Canadian Peacebuilding Initiative. Because peace-building lies at the inter-section of international security and development, the Initiative is a joint undertaking of Canada's Department of Foreign Affairs and International Trade (DFAIT) and CIDA. It has two objectives: to assist countries in conflict in their efforts toward peace and stability, and to promote Canadian capacity and participation in international peacebuilding initiatives.

A key goal of the Peacebuilding Initiative is to improve co-ordination among international actors. This involves strengthening the UN's capacity to prevent conflict, to respond rapidly when conflict erupts and to provide for post-conflict reconstruction.

Under the Initiative, Canada has worked to improve UN capacity to respond to these challenges. Among other things, it has contributed to the UN Trust Fund for Preventive Action and the Trust Fund for Children and Armed Conflict, and has promoted strengthening the role of Special Representatives of the Secretary-General, and the conflict prevention capacity of regional organizations and the UN itself. Canada has also supported the UN Lessons Learned Unit to develop guidelines for demilitarization, demobi-lization and re-integration of combatants in post-conflict situations. At home, Canada has developed a national roster of Canadian civilians who are available on short notice to provide assistance and expertise to international peace support operations organized by the UN and regional organizations.

Closely linked to Canada's efforts to promote peacebuilding is its work to marshal international support for the concept of human security. While traditional approaches to international relations have focussed on the security of states and territory as ends in themselves, human security recognizes that in today's world there are many new threats to the safety and security of people. Small arms proliferation, international drug trafficking and organized crime, environmental degradation, and civil conflict are only some of the threats that extend beyond borders and require truly international solutions. With its two-year term on the Security Council, Canada is striving to expand the UN's role in addressing human security issues, such as the proliferation of small arms, the protection of children in armed conflict and the toll of modern conflict on civilians.

Non-proliferation, arms control and disarmament

As we seek new tools for the UN to respond to threats to security, we must not relax our efforts in traditional areas of concern, such as non-proliferation, arms control and disarmament. With the indefinite extension of the Nuclear Non-Proliferation Treaty in 1995 and the opening for signature of the Comprehensive Test-Ban Treaty in 1996, the international

community took a historic and definitive step forward on nuclear disarmament. Canada is firmly committed to pursuing the goal set out in the Test-Ban Treaty of reducing and ultimately eliminating nuclear weapons.

We are equally concerned that there be no relaxation in the international condemnation of chemical and biological weapons, and in support for treaties dealing with them. Nor should the international community neglect the threats to security arising from excessive and destabilizing accumulations of conventional weapons. We believe that more can and should be done at the multilateral level to address such concerns, including issues related to small arms and light weapons.

Elimination of anti-personnel mines

A deadly legacy of conflicts that may have ended decades before, anti-personnel mines victimize more than 20 000 people every year. Most of the casualties are civilians, many of them children, and almost all live in developing countries.

That is why, in October 1996, Canada hosted the Ottawa Conference entitled "Toward a Global Ban on Anti-Personnel Mines," bringing together more than 70 states to discuss a strategy for achieving a global landmine ban. In the Ottawa Declaration, participating states committed to ensuring "the earliest possible conclusion of a legally binding international agreement to ban anti-personnel landmines." Determined to see this unprecedented

CIDA photo: Roger LeMoyne

gathering produce speedy action, Canada's Minister of Foreign Affairs, Lloyd Axworthy, invited the participants to return to Canada's capital one year later to sign a global treaty banning landmines. Some 122 countries accepted the invitation and signed the Ottawa Convention on December 3 and 4, 1997. It became the most rapidly ratified international treaty ever when it came into force on March 1, 1999.

Canada is proud of the momentum created through the Ottawa Process toward a global ban on landmines. To act on its commitment, it has pledged $100 million over five years to create the Canadian Landmine Fund, which is being used to further the goals of the Ottawa Convention (Section 6). For regular updates on Canadian mine action, visit the Safe Lane Web site at **www.mines.gc.ca**.

Economic and social development

Sustainable development is a cornerstone of Canadian foreign policy. Canada sees the United Nations and the UN funds, programmes and specialized agencies (where it plays a leading role) as key instruments for promoting economic and social development. Canada was and is very active in the UN reform process; we want the administrative savings achieved by the different funds and programmes to be applied as "development dividends" to finance the alleviation of poverty and economic growth generation in developing countries.

Through bilateral assistance and participation in UN funds, programmes

CIDA photo: David Barbour

and institutions, as well as in the regional development banks, Canada has supported African development for many years. We have been a leading player in addressing the problem of debt: we were among the first to forgive the official development assistance (ODA) debt of the least-developed and other poor countries, and were equally prompt in reducing the debts of the poorest highly-indebted countries. We have a long tradition of development assistance in Asia and are active partners in building new forms of co-operation in the Asia–Pacific Economic Cooperation (APEC) forum and other regional forums. Further, Canada is a full partner in Latin American and Caribbean development, and we maintain an active program of assistance to Central and Eastern Europe and the former Soviet Union in order to assist in their transition to democracy and market economies.

Environment

Solving environmental problems is a top international priority for Canadians. Canada is a leader on the issue of biodiversity, and was one of the first countries to ratify the Convention on Biological Diversity. Montréal was chosen as the site for the Permanent Secretariat of the Convention.

At the United Nations Conference on Environment and Development in 1992, Canada played a strong role in developing the Forest Principles. Since then, Canada has launched the International Model Forest Programme, the Montréal Criteria and Indicators Process, and the Intergovernmental Working Group on Forests (co-sponsored with Malaysia), and was an active participant in the Intergovernmental Panel on Forests, sponsored by the UN Commission on Sustainable Development. Canada is also a proponent of a legally binding instrument on sustainable forest management.

In addition, Canada has been a key player in international ocean issues. Over the past three decades, Canada has provided approximately $600 million worth of assistance to developing countries to help them sustainably develop their fisheries. Canada has supported the drafting of an Ocean Charter, which has now been endorsed by UNESCO, and was instrumental in securing the UN Agreement on Straddling Stocks and Highly Migratory Stocks. This agreement focusses on the conservation and sustainable utilization of fisheries resources.

Canada played an active role in the negotiations leading to the UN Convention to Combat Desertification. Canada considers desertification to be both a developmental and environmental problem. It is providing $800 million in bilateral desertification-related programs, aside from multilateral and partnership funding.

All of these measures are necessary if the international community and our international institutions are to keep pace with the changing nature of global environmental problems.

CIDA photo: Roger LeMoyne

Human rights

Since the end of the Second World War, Canada has been a consistently strong voice in the world's councils for the protection of human rights and the defence of democratic values. From the drafting of the Universal Declaration of Human Rights over 50 years ago through actions taken in a vast range of forums and circumstances, Canada has always been there.

Canada is an active participant in the annual meetings of the UN Commission on Human Rights in Geneva, and it regularly co-sponsors a number of resolutions. Sometimes these are on specific countries where the human rights situation is particularly serious. They may also be on issues Canada feels strongly about, such as violence against women, freedom of expression or impunity.

Other Canadian initiatives have included efforts to ensure consideration of human rights issues in all UN activities, leadership in establishing the position of UNHCHR, and support for the increasing number of human rights field operations of the Office of the High Commissioner for Human Rights, including units attached to UN peacekeeping operations.

Canada also played a significant role in establishing the International Criminal Court. It actively took part in the preparatory discussions and chaired the June 1998 international negotiating conference. Canada's contribution helped bring about an international court in which to try cases of genocide, crimes against humanity and other war crimes.

Canada plays a major role as well in the preparation, debates and follow-up of various UN world conferences concerned with human rights—for example, the 1993 Vienna World Conference on Human Rights and the upcoming 2001 Conference on Racism.

As a signatory of all the principal UN treaties on international human rights, Canada regularly submits its human rights record to review by UN monitoring bodies.

By working through the Canadian International Development Agency, via bilateral assistance as well as participation in the UN funds, programmes and special institutions, Canada continues to help

CIDA photo: Roger LeMoyne

societies build human rights capacity through strengthening the electoral process, the judicial system, legislatures and independent media.

Women

Canada is committed to drawing attention to violations of the human rights of women. On International Women's Day, March 8, 1993, the Commission on Human Rights adopted by consensus a first-ever resolution, introduced by Canada, aimed at integrating the rights of women into the UN human rights mechanisms.

Canadian efforts have also sought to gain recognition that violence against women is a breach of human rights. Canada helped draft the UN Declaration on the Elimination of Violence against Women, adopted by the General Assembly in December 1993. In 1994, Canada was behind the Commission on Human Rights' creation of the post of Special Rapporteur on violence against women.

Children

A Canadian priority, and a key element in our efforts to improve human security, is strengthening respect for children's rights, particularly by eliminating exploitative child labour, the sexual exploitation of children, the widespread use of child soldiers and the victimization of children in armed conflict.

At the multilateral and bilateral levels, Canada is working in partnership with

CIDA photo: Ron Watts

developing countries to protect children, strengthen their rights and assist victims of the sex trade. Canada supports the negotiations of an International Labour Organization (ILO) convention on the elimination of exploitation of child labour, and it also supports the ILO's International Programme for the Elimination of Exploitation of Child Labour.

Indigenous peoples

In partnership with like-minded states and organizations of Indigenous peoples, Canada is working hard at the UN to promote and protect the human rights, well-being and sustainable development of Indigenous peoples. At the Working Group on the Draft UN Declaration on the Rights of Indigenous Peoples, Canada has played a lead role with a view to achieving adoption of the Declaration by the UN General Assembly before the end of the International Decade of the World's Indigenous People in 2004. Canada supports the establishment of a permanent forum for Indigenous peoples within the UN system; this is another major goal of the International Decade.

UN reform

Over 50 years after its creation, the forces of globalization have presented the United Nations with challenges and pressures unimagined by its founders. As we enter the 21st century, Canada believes we need to re-invent and not merely restructure the United Nations in order to ensure that it remains credible and relevant to the lives of individuals.

Renewing the United Nations: A Programme for Reform, a document presented by Secretary-General Kofi Annan before the United Nations General Assembly in July 1997, proposes the most extensive and far-reaching reforms in the 54-year history of the international body. The reform process should help enhance the credibility and effectiveness of the UN. Canada's reform efforts at the UN have focussed on making the United Nations more effective, not simply less expensive. These efforts include simplifying the structure of the UN Secretariat services involved in development, strengthening the Economic and Social Council, reducing overlap in UN specialized agencies, reviewing the UN's funds and programmes to ensure better co-ordination of their activities in the field, and streamlining the UN machinery in the economic and social fields so that the efficiency savings achieved may be devoted to the UN's development activities.

Main Funds and
Programmes of the
United Nations

Main Funds and Programmes of the United Nations

International Research and Training Institute for the Advancement of Women

César Nicolás Pensón 102-A
Santo Domingo
Dominican Republic
Tel.: (809) 685-2111
Fax: (809) 685-2117
E-mail: instraw.hq.sd@codetel.net.do
Web site: www.un.org/instraw
Director: Yakin Erturk (Turkey)

The International Research and Training Institute for the Advancement of Women (INSTRAW) was created in 1976 to conduct policy research and develop international training programs in order to: *(a)* help emancipate women; *(b)* help them participate more actively and equitably in development; *(c)* raise awareness of gender equality issues; and *(d)* create global networks to help make gender equality a reality.

The Institute, an autonomous body within the United Nations system, is funded exclusively through voluntary contributions from UN member states, intergovernmental agencies, non-governmental organizations, philanthropic institutions and individuals.

International Trade Centre UNCTAD/WTO

Palais des Nations
CH-1211, Geneva 10, Switzerland
Tel.: (41-22) 730-111
Fax: (41-22) 733-4439
Telex: 414 119 ITC CH
E-mail: itcreg@intracen.org
Web site: www.intracen.org
Executive Director: J. Denis Bélisle (Canada)

The International Trade Centre UNCTAD/WTO (ITC) was founded in 1964 by the forerunner of the World Trade Organization, the General Agreement on Tariffs and Trade (GATT). Four years later, the United Nations Conference on Trade and Development joined with the GATT in assuming operation of the Centre. ITC's role is to work with developing nations and economies in transition to help them introduce effective trade promotion programs with a view to increasing their exports and improving control over their imports.

ITC concentrates its energies in six sectors, including product and market development and human resources development, in order to enhance the effectiveness of developing countries' trade activities.

Joint United Nations Programme on HIV/AIDS

20, avenue Appia
CH-1211, Geneva 27, Switzerland
Tel.: (41-22) 791-3666
Fax: (41-22) 791-4187
E-mail: unaids@unaids.org
Web site: www.unaids.org
Executive Director: Peter Piot (Belgium)

On January 1, 1996, the Joint United Nations Programme on HIV/AIDS (UNAIDS) was created by the General Assembly acting on a resolution adopted during the 1993 World Health Assembly. The Programme is co-administered by six specialized UN agencies, including the World Health Organization and the World Bank.

UNAIDS seeks to direct, strengthen and support the international community's efforts to prevent the transmission of the AIDS virus, provide care and support to victims and caregivers, reduce individuals' and communities' vulnerability to AIDS, and lessen the impact of the current epidemic.

United Nations Centre for Human Settlements (Habitat)

United Nations Avenue, Gigiri
Nairobi, Kenya
Tel.: (254-2) 621-234
Fax: (254-2) 624-266
E-mail: habitat@unchs.org
Web site: www.habitat.org
or: www.unchs.org
Acting Executive Director:
Klaus Töpfer (Germany)

Founded in 1978, the United Nations Centre for Human Settlements, or UNCHS (Habitat), is the main co-ordinating agency for all human settlement development activities within the extended UN family. UNCHS (Habitat) promotes sustainable development of human settlements through appropriate policies, knowledge development, and stronger partnerships between governments and civil society.

The Centre currently runs over 200 programs and projects in 80 countries, dealing with urban management, housing, basic services and infrastructure development.

CIDA photo: David Barbour

United Nations Children's Fund

UNICEF House
3 United Nations Plaza
New York, NY 10017, United States
Tel.: (212) 326-7000
Fax: (212) 888-7465
E-mail: webmaster@unicef.org
Web site: www.unicef.org
Director: Carol Bellamy (United States)

UNICEF was set up as the United Nations International Children's Emergency Fund in 1946 at the very first session of the General Assembly. Its mission was to provide emergency help to child victims of the Second World War. In 1953, its mission was extended to meeting the long-term needs of children in developing countries. At that time its name was changed to the United Nations Children's Fund to reflect its wider mandate.

UNICEF is the only UN organization devoted exclusively to children's issues.

It works and speaks out for children's rights with a view to helping the world's young meet their basic needs and improve their chances of realizing their full potential. The Fund works with other organs in the United Nations system, with governments and with non-governmental organizations in 161 countries and territories. The aim is to lighten children's burden through community services offering primary health care, basic education, clean water and public health in developing countries.

UNICEF is funded entirely by voluntary contributions from governments, non-governmental organizations, the private sector, other UN agencies and individuals. In 1997, total contributions to UNICEF exceeded US$900 million.

UNICEF was awarded the Nobel Peace Prize in 1965.

United Nations Conference on Trade and Development

Palais des Nations
CH-1211, Geneva 10, Switzerland
Tel.: (41-22) 907-1234
Fax: (41-22) 907-0057
Telex: 412962
E-mail: webmaster@unctad.org
Web site: www.unctad.org
Secretary-General: Rubens Ricupero
(Brazil)

Established in 1964, the United Nations Conference on Trade and Development (UNCTAD) is the UN's main organ in the field of trade and development. It is the driving force behind the United Nations

system's integrated approach to development problems and to the closely related issues of trade, funding, technology, investment and sustainable development.

Its main objectives are to help Third World countries so that they can get the most out of the trade, investment and development opportunities available to them, come to terms with the problems stemming from globalization, and carve out their rightful place in the world economy.

More specifically, UNCTAD—with its 188 member states—assists developing countries, especially the least-developed ones, in deriving maximum benefit from globalization, becoming well integrated into the international trading system, increasing their export capacity, diversifying their commodity production, managing their debt, attracting capital, improving investment conditions and strengthening their technological capacities.

UNCTAD works in close co-operation with a host of other organizations in the United Nations system, including the World Trade Organization, the World Bank and the International Monetary Fund, as well as with a wide range of private and public agencies at both the national and international levels.

United Nations Development Fund for Women

304 East 45th Street, 6th Floor
New York, NY 10017, United States
Tel.: (212) 906-6400
Fax: (212) 906-6705
E-mail: unifem@undp.org
Web site: www.unifem.undp.org
Director: Noeleen Heyzer (Singapore)

An independent organization working closely with the United Nations Development Programme, the United Nations Development Fund for Women (UNIFEM) was created in 1984 by the UN

General Assembly in order to promote the economic and political emancipation of women in the developing world. Since 1997, UNIFEM has also assisted women in Central and East European countries.

UNIFEM seeks to ensure participation by women in every stage of the development process, and to act as a catalyst within the United Nations system in efforts to link women's needs and concerns with all questions of critical interest to them at the global, national and regional levels.

United Nations Development Programme

1 United Nations Plaza
New York, NY 10017, United States
Tel.: (212) 906-5000
Fax: (212) 906-5364
Telex: 125980, 422862
E-mail: hq@undp.org
Web site: www.undp.org
Administrator: Mark Malloch Brown
(United Kingdom)

The United Nations Development Programme (UNDP) began operating in 1966. This is the United Nations system's main technical co-operation and

co-ordination program. UNDP's chief objective is to help countries help themselves achieve people-focussed sustainable development. It is active in poverty eradication, job creation, women's advancement and restoration of the environment. In addition, UNDP is increasingly asked to provide assistance in organizing democratic elections, and to support postconflict reconciliation and reconstruction.

UNDP's operations are decentralized. It funds projects in over 170 countries through a network of 132 local offices. At the national level, each UNDP office director is generally appointed the resident United Nations system co-ordinator for operational development activities. UNDP-funded activities are carried out in large part by the recipient countries themselves, in keeping with the principle of capacity development; but if needed, UN specialized agencies or non-governmental organizations will contribute services.

UNDP's Board of Directors is made up of 36 member states, including 12 industrialized countries. Canada is currently a member of the Board.

Since 1990, UNDP has become a major promoter of ideas through its annual *Human Development Report.* The 1998 edition again ranked Canada first on the human development index, for the fifth consecutive year.

United Nations Environment Programme

P.O. Box 30552
United Nations Avenue, Gigiri
Nairobi, Kenya
Tel.: (254-2) 621-234, 520-600
Fax: (254-2) 226-886 or 226-890
Telex: 22068, 22173
E-mail: unepinfo@unep.org
Web site: www.unep.org
Executive Director: Klaus Töpfer
(Germany)

Founded in 1972, the United Nations Environment Programme (UNEP) seeks to provide international leadership and encourage partnerships dedicated to

protecting the environment. UNEP co-ordinates UN environmental activities, monitors changes in the environment, conducts research, holds seminars and offers training programs on environmental protection.

The Programme advises and aids developing nations on environmental aspects of development. It promotes sustainable development, i.e., economic development that improves the quality of life of people today without compromising that of future generations.

CIDA photo: Peter Bennett

United Nations High Commissioner for Human Rights

Palais des Nations
8-14, avenue de la Paix
CH-1211, Geneva 10, Switzerland
Tel.: (41-22) 917-3134
Fax: (41-22) 917-0245
E-mail: secrt.hchr@unog.ch
Web site: www.unhchr.ch
High Commissioner: Mary Robinson
(Ireland)

In 1993 the General Assembly created the position of UN High Commissioner for Human Rights (UNHCHR), the aim being to promote and protect the full exercise by all individuals of all civil, cultural, economic, political and social rights, including the right to development. The High Commissioner is also responsible for all UN human rights activities, including the Commission on Human Rights.

The High Commissioner co-ordinates all activities in this sphere by organizations in the United Nations system, tries to prevent infringements on basic rights, investigates those that do occur and works with governments to remedy such situations.

United Nations High Commissioner for Refugees

94, rue Montbrillant
CH-1211, Geneva 2, Switzerland
Tel.: (41-22) 739-8111
Fax: (41-22) 731-9546
Telex: 41 57 40 UNHCR CH
E-mail: webmaster@unhcr.ch
Web site: www.unhcr.ch
High Commissioner: Sadako Ogata
(Japan)

The Office of the United Nations High Commissioner for Refugees (UNHCR) was founded in 1950 and began operating on January 1, 1951, taking over from the International Refugee Organization. The UNHCR was mandated to assist people who had been uprooted from their homes during and after the Second World War. Thanks to the adoption of the Convention on the Status of Refugees in July 1951, UNHCR was able to help refugees find safe havens and offer them the opportunity to rebuild their lives. Before the Convention, such people at most could apply to emigrate to another country. If they were refused, they had no recourse and no way of ensuring their own safety.

UNHCR's work is humanitarian and non-political. Its main functions are to offer refugees international protection, seek lasting solutions to their problems and provide them with material assistance in the form of food, shelter, medical assistance, education and other social services.

The Office of the High Commissioner seeks to help refugees wishing to return to their country of origin and become re-integrated into their communities. When this is unfeasible, UNHCR tries to assist them in their country of refuge or to find them a new host country.

The convention governing UNHCR's activities excludes, however, people guilty of crimes against peace, war crimes or crimes against humanity. Also excluded from any UNHCR assistance are people who have committed serious non-political crimes outside the country in which refuge is sought, as well as those who are guilty of acts contrary to the purposes and principles of the UN.

According to conservative estimates, there are currently over 15 million refugees within the meaning of the Convention on the Status of Refugees ("Convention refugees"). Canada is a prime destination for those seeking refuge and asylum. Since 1959, it is estimated that Canada has accepted slightly over 500 000 refugees from around the world. In recent years, however, Canada has tightened its admission criteria to allow only true Convention refugees.

United Nations Institute for Disarmament Research

Palais des Nations
CH-1211, Geneva 10, Switzerland
Tel.: (41-22) 917-3186 or 917-4293
Fax: (41-22) 917-0176
Telex: 412962
E-mail: plewis@unog.ch or ccarle@unog.ch
Web site: www.unog.ch/unidir
Director: Patricia Lewis (United Kingdom)

Established in 1980 by the General Assembly, the United Nations Institute for Disarmament Research (UNIDIR) is mandated to carry out independent research on disarmament and other questions dealing with international security. By means of this research, the Institute provides the international community with complete data on problems associated with international security, the arms race and disarmament, with a particular emphasis on nuclear weapons, so as to strengthen the movement toward enhanced security for all states. The Institute is also responsible for supporting the negotiations on disarmament by providing the participants with factual studies and objective analyses.

CIDA photo: Virginia Boyd

United Nations Office for Drug Control and Crime Prevention

Vienna International Centre
Wagramerstrasse 5, P.O. Box 500
A-1400, Vienna, Austria
Tel.: (43-1) 213-450
Fax: (43-1) 213-455866
Telex: 135612
E-mail: undcp_hq@undcp.un.or.at
Web site: www.odccp.org
Executive Director: Pino Arlacchi (Italy)

The United Nations Office for Drug Control and Crime Prevention (ODCCP) was created on November 1, 1997, to allow the United Nations to focus its energies and enhance its capacity for dealing with the interrelated problems of drugs, crime and international terrorism. It comprises the United Nations International Drug Control Programme (UNDCP), which was established to provide a world centre of expertise and information on international narcotics control, and the Centre for International Crime Prevention (CICP).

UNDCP co-ordinates and directs all UN activities in this area, employing experts from around the world and disseminating information on substance abuse. It also provides governments with technical assistance to help them accede to international drug control treaties and implement them once ratified.

CICP co-ordinates all UN activities in the field of crime prevention and criminal justice, paying spccial attention to transnational organized crime, illicit trafficking in human beings, economic crime and terrorism.

United Nations Population Fund

220 East 42nd Street
New York, NY 10017, United States
Tel.: (212) 297-5020
Fax: (212) 557-6416
Telex: 422031 or 422038
E-mail: ryaxuv@unfpa.org
Web site: www.unfpa.org
Executive Director: Nafis Sadik (Pakistan)

Founded in 1967, the United Nations Population Fund (UNFPA) provides assistance to developing nations, countries in transition and any other country that requests help in dealing with population and reproductive health issues, and in raising awareness of these issues around the world.

UNFPA is active in three main areas: (1) promotion of universal access by the year 2015 for all couples and individuals to reproductive health care—in particular, family planning and sexual health; (2) support for population and development strategies aimed at strengthening population planning capabilities; and (3) raising awareness of population and development issues.

In addition, UNFPA—guided by the Programme of Action of the International Conference on Population and Development, held in Cairo in September 1994—is committed to promoting reproductive rights, gender equality, men's responsibilities, and women's autonomy and emancipation throughout the world.

United Nations Relief and Works Agency for Palestine Refugees in the Near East

UNRWA Headquarters (Amman, Jordan)
Bayader Wadi Seer, P.O. Box 140157
Amman 11814, Jordan
Tel.: (962-6) 826-171/6
Fax: (962-6) 864-149

UNRWA Headquarters (Gaza)
Gamal Abdul Nasser Street, P.O. Box 371
Gaza City
or
P.O. Box 338, Ashqelon 78100, Israel
Tel.: (972-7) 677-7700
Fax: (972-7) 677-7555
Commissioner-General: Peter Hansen
(Denmark)

The United Nations Relief and Works Agency for Palestine Refugees in the Near East (UNRWA) was created in 1949 and commenced operations on May 1, 1950. Its original mission was, in co-operation with the host countries, to provide emergency relief to some 750 000 people, mostly Palestinian Arabs, who had lost their homes and all their possessions during the conflict between Israel and its Arab neighbours in 1948. Subsequently, its mandate was broadened to include the victims of the 1967 war.

UNRWA provides emergency relief, health care services and educational services to needy Palestinian refugees in Gaza, the West Bank, Jordan, Lebanon and Syria. By December 1997, UNRWA was providing essential services to nearly 3.5 million refugees, a third of whom were living in 59 different refugee camps.

United Nations University

53-70 Jingumae 5-chome, Shibuya-ku
Tokyo 150, Japan
Tel.: (81-3) 349-92811
Fax: (81-3) 349-92828
Telex: J25442 UNAT UNIV
E-mail: mbox@hq.unu.edu
Web site: www.unu.edu
Rector: Hans van Ginkel (Netherlands)

The United Nations University (UNU) was established in 1975. Funded entirely through donations from governments, agencies, foundations and individuals, UNU focusses on research, postgraduate studies and the dissemination of knowledge on critical areas of concern, such as human survival, development and well-being. The University has its headquarters in Tokyo, Japan, but also operates five research and training centres in Finland, the Netherlands, Macau, Ghana and Japan. In addition, UNU runs three specialized programs, including the International Network on Water, Environment and Health in Hamilton, Ontario.

United Nations Volunteers

Haus Carstanjen
Martin Luther King Strasse, 8
Bonn-Plittersdorf
Mailing address: Postfach 260111
D-53153, Bonn, Germany
Tel.: (49-228) 815-2000
Fax: (49-228) 815-2001
E-mail: enquiry@unv.org
Web site: www.unv.org
Executive Co-ordinator:
Sharon Capeling-Alakija (Canada)

The United Nations Volunteers (UNV), a program created in 1971, is one of the UN's crowning achievements. In 1997 these volunteers numbered over 3600 women and men, with an average age of about 40. Drawn from 115 occupational categories, they worked in 147 countries, including the 48 least developed.

Assignments are for a two-year period, and the volunteers work in five main fields: (1) technical co-operation; (2) assistance to non-governmental organizations and community groups wishing to set up local development projects; (3) humanitarian aid and social re-integration; (4) support for UN operations involving peacebuilding, conflict resolution, human rights and democratic process; and (5) development of entrepreneurship in the private and public sectors.

Volunteers are sent to countries only at their request and with their approval. The projects involve all sectors of activity, from health and education to environmental protection, agriculture, fisheries and forestry.

World Food Programme

Via Cesare Giulio Viola 68-70
Parco de Medici
00148, Rome, Italy
Tel.: (39-06) 651-31
Fax: (39-06) 596-0632/637
Telex: 626675 WFP
E-mail: nom@wfp.org
Web site: www.wfp.org
Executive Director: Catherine Bertini
(United States)

The World Food Programme (WFP) was founded in 1963 and has its head-quarters in Rome. It is the United Nations agency responsible for food aid. The world's leading international organization of this type, the WFP uses food aid to:

- save human lives in humanitarian crises;

- assist the most vulnerable, especially women and children, when it is essential to meet their food needs in order to allow them to better realize their full human potential; and

- help people suffering from hunger to achieve self-dependence, and equip their communities with vital infrastructure such as roads, schools and irrigation systems.

Specialized Agencies of the
United Nations

Specialized Agencies of the United Nations

Food and Agriculture Organization

Viale delle Terme di Caracalla
00100 Rome, Italy
Tel.: (39-6) 570-51
Fax: (39-6) 570-53152
Telex: 625852 FAO 1
E-mail: gii-registry@fao.org
Web site: www.fao.org
Director-General: Jacques Diouf
        (Senegal)

The Food and Agriculture Organization of the United Nations (FAO) came into existence in October 1945 in Québec City—the first specialized agency within the UN. Its mandate is to enhance nutrition levels, living standards, agricultural productivity and rural living conditions.

Since its inception, FAO, which has 175 member states, has fought world hunger and poverty by promoting agricultural development, nutritional quality and food security. It seeks to give people everywhere access at all times to the food they need to lead active, healthy lives. The Organization provides direct support for development; it gathers, analyses and disseminates information; it offers governments policy and planning advice; and it serves as a global forum for discussing agricultural and food issues.

FAO emphasizes sustainable rural development and agriculture. It is active on a number of fronts: land and water development, crop and animal production, forests, fisheries, economic and social policy, investment, nutrition, food standards, commodities, and trade. Last, FAO plays an active role in dealing with agricultural and food crises.

CIDA photo: Peter Bennett

International Atomic Energy Agency

Vienna International Centre
Wagramerstrasse 5, P.O. Box 100
A-1400, Vienna, Austria
Tel.: (43-1) 26000
Fax: (43-1) 26007
Telex: 1-12645
E-mail: official.mail@iaea.org
Web site: www.iaea.org
Director-General: Mohamed El Baradei
(Egypt)

The International Atomic Energy Agency (IAEA) acts as a global central intergovernmental forum for scientific and technical co-operation in the field of nuclear energy, and as an international inspection agency for compliance with protection standards and verification measures covering civil nuclear programs.

Created in 1957, the Agency has 128 member states. It has offices in Canada, Geneva, New York and Tokyo, and operates laboratories in Austria and Monaco, as well as a research centre in Trieste, Italy. IAEA deploys about 200 inspectors throughout the world to monitor nearly 1000 facilities and other sites that come under its Protection Programme.

International Civil Aviation Organization

999 University Street
Montréal, Quebec H3C 5H7
Canada
Tel.: (514) 954-8219
Fax: (514) 954-6077
Telex: 05 24513
E-mail: icaohq@iaco.org
Web site: www.icao.int
President of the Council: Assad Kotaite
(Lebanon)
Secretary-General: R.C. Costa Pereira
(Brazil)

The International Civil Aviation Organization (ICAO) was created in Chicago on December 7, 1944, when 52 countries signed the Convention on International Civil Aviation. It officially came into existence on April 4, 1947. The Organization, which now has 185 member states, is the specialized agency responsible for developing the rules and regulations governing all aspects of civil aviation, including air corridors, safety, environmental standards for aircraft, and training for flight and ground personnel.

ICAO works closely with several other UN specialized agencies, such as the World Meteorological Organization and the International Telecommunications Union, as well as a number of non-governmental organizations, including the International Air Transport Association, the Airports Council International and the International Federation of Air Line Pilots' Associations.

There are over 40 000 civil airports in the world today and some 10 000 aircraft, including 5000 passenger aircraft (the majority in North America) in the air at any given time.

International Fund for Agricultural Development

107, via del Serafico
00142 Rome, Italy
Tel.: (39-6) 545-91
Fax: (39-6) 504-3463
Telex: 620330 IFAD
E-mail: ifad@ifad.org
Web site: www.ifad.org
President: Fawzi Al-Sultan (Kuwait)

Created in 1977, the International Fund for Agricultural Development (IFAD), which has 161 member states, grew out of the 1974 World Food Conference. The Conference had been organized to find solutions to the food crises of the early 1970s, particularly in the countries of sub-Saharan Africa. The aim of the Fund is to combat rural hunger and poverty in developing nations. IFAD's programs focus on small agricultural producers, landless peasants, nomadic shepherds and rural women living in poverty.

Since its inception, the Fund has financed nearly 500 projects in 111 countries, for a total of approximately US$6 billion. To this figure must be added the contributions of the recipient countries (close to US$6.5 billion), and of donor countries and multilateral agencies (US$5.5 billion). These projects, which are aimed at stimulating food production, have given help to almost 200 million people.

International Labour Organization

4, route des Morillons
CH-1211, Geneva 22, Switzerland
Tel.: (41-22) 799-6111
Fax: (41-22) 798-8685
Telex: 41 56 47
E-mail: webinfo@hql.ilo.ch
Web site: www.ilo.org
Director-General: Juan Somavía (Chile)

Created in 1919 by the Treaty of Versailles, the International Labour Organization (ILO) is mandated to promote social justice and respect for workers' rights throughout the world. It became a UN specialized agency in 1946.

The ILO develops international labour conventions and recommendations that set the minimum standards to be followed in the areas under its mandate: freedom of association, the right to organize, collective bargaining rights, the abolition of forced labour, equality of opportunity and treatment, etc. It offers technical assistance in various sectors: vocational training and rehabilitation, employment policy, labour administration, labour law, staff relations, working conditions, management training, co-operatives, social security, labour statistics, and occupational health and safety. The ILO encourages the creation of independent employer and labour organizations, and facilitates their growth through training activities and advice.

Within the UN system, the ILO is unique by virtue of its tripartite structure: employers and workers participate in the activities of its governing bodies on an equal footing with governments. On the occasion of its 50th anniversary in 1969, the ILO was awarded the Nobel Peace Prize.

International Maritime Organization

4 Albert Embankment
London SE1 7SR, United Kingdom
Tel.: (44-171) 735-7611
Fax: (44-171) 587-3210
Telex: 235-88 (CALL BACK: IMOLDN G)
E-mail: info@imo.org
Web site: www.imo.org
Secretary-General: William A. O'Neil
(Canada)

The international convention creating the International Maritime Organization (IMO) was adopted in 1948 in Geneva, but it was not until 1958 that the Organization officially began operating. The IMO held its first meeting the following year. It has a staff of only 300, making it one of the smallest agencies in the United Nations system. The Organization has 155 member states.

The IMO's mandate is to improve safety at sea and control marine pollution caused by ships. Its first order of business, which it carried out in 1960, was to adopt a new version of the International Convention for the Safety of Life at Sea (SOLAS Convention), the primary instrument for marine safety. Since then, the Organization has focussed on a number of issues, including the facilitation of international maritime traffic, the transportation of hazardous goods and efforts to end unfair trade practices by shipping concerns.

International Monetary Fund

700 19th Street NW
Washington, DC 20431
United States
Tel.: (202) 623-7000
Fax: (202) 623-4661
E-mail: publicaffairs@imf.org or
(firstname).(lastname)@imf.org
Web site: www.imf.org
Managing Director: Michel Camdessus
(France)

The International Monetary Fund (IMF) is one of the major institutions that grew out of the 1944 Bretton Woods Agreement. The creation of the IMF, which now has 182 member states, resulted from the international community's efforts to develop an effective monetary system in order to avoid a repetition of such economic crises as the Great Depression of the 1930s, which ruined millions of people around the world.

The IMF works closely with the World Bank. Its original mandate was to bring stability to currency exchange rates and discipline to the international monetary system, to promote international trade and capital flows, and to support high rates of sustainable economic growth. The IMF has become the central institution of the international monetary system. It oversees the economic policies of member states, provides economic and financial advice, and gives short- and medium-term financial assistance to countries facing balance of payments problems and other difficulties.

The IMF is funded by the annual contributions of its members, prorated according to their gross domestic product and adjusted every five years. The sums held by the Fund—close to US$287 billion—are used to grant loans to members in financial difficulty. The IMF's other main function is to co-ordinate its members' efforts to achieve greater international co-operation in setting economic policy.

Canada is the eighth-biggest contributor to the IMF, after the six other G-7 countries and Saudi Arabia.

International Telecommunications Union

Place des Nations
CH-1211, Geneva 20, Switzerland
Tel.: (41-22) 730-5111
Fax: (41-22) 733-7256
E-mail: itumail@itu.int
Web site: www.itu.int
Secretary-General: Yoshio Itsumi
(Japan)

The very first international telecommunications agreement dates back to May 17, 1865, barely 21 years after Samuel Morse invented the telegraph. On that date 20 countries signed the International Telegraph Convention and created the International Telegraph Union, the forerunner of the International Telecommunications Union (ITU). The ITU became a UN specialized agency on October 15, 1947.

The ITU is responsible for assigning all television and radio frequencies around the world through a very strict system. The Union also co-ordinates all forms of international telecommunications and is involved in the assignment of orbits for telecommunications satellites.

Since 1989, with the creation of the Telecommunications Development Bureau, the ITU has devoted considerable effort to helping developing countries adopt modern telecommunications structures and thereby take full advantage of all the latest technological breakthroughs.

United Nations Educational, Scientific and Cultural Organization

7, Place de Fontenay
F-75732, Paris 07 SP, France
Tel.: (33-1) 456-81000
Fax: (33-1) 456-71690
Telex: 204461
E-mail: info@unesco.org
Web site: www.unesco.org
Director-General: Federico Mayor Zaragoza
(Spain)

Founded on November 16, 1945, the United Nations Educational, Scientific and Cultural Organization (UNESCO) currently has 186 member states. Its main objective is to help maintain global peace and security by fostering greater co-operation between nations through education, science, culture and communication. In so doing, UNESCO aims to ensure universal respect for justice, law, human rights and fundamental freedoms for all irrespective of race, gender, language or religion.

UNESCO works to combat illiteracy, advance the spread of scientific knowledge and increase mutual understanding between the peoples of the world through educational and cultural exchanges, as well as through respect for justice and the rule of law.

Last, UNESCO contributes to the maintenance, advancement and dissemination of knowledge by: *(a)* seeing to the conservation and protection of our universal heritage consisting of books, works of art, and other monuments of historical or scientific interest; *(b)* promoting co-operation between nations in all branches of intellectual activity, as well as international exchanges of representatives in the fields of education, science and culture, plus exchange of publications, works of art, laboratory equipment and any useful documentation; and *(c)* through appropriate methods of international co-operation, facilitating access by all peoples to the publications of each.

United Nations Industrial Development Organization

Vienna International Centre
Wagramerstrasse 5, P.O. Box 300
A-1400, Vienna, Austria
Tel.: (43-1) 260-26
Fax: (43-1) 269-2669
Telex: 135612 UNO A
Cable: UNIDO VIENNA
E-mail: unido-pinfo@unido.org
Web site: www.unido.org
Director-General: Carlos Magariños
(Argentina)

The United Nations Industrial Development Organization (UNIDO) was created in 1966 by the UN General Assembly, but it was not until 1985 that it became a full-fledged agency of the United Nations. The Organization, which has 168 member states, helps less-developed nations establish new industries or improve existing ones.

More specifically, UNIDO's role is to assist developing countries and economies in transition in adopting a sustainable industrial development structure. To fulfil this mandate, UNIDO offers them solutions geared to their needs and their situation, through a series of integrated services addressing three main concerns: *(a)* a competitive economy; *(b)* a healthy environment; and *(c)* a high level of productivity in terms of policies, institutions and businesses.

CIDA photo: David Barbour

Universal Postal Union

Weltpoststrasse 4
P.O. Box 3000, Berne 15, Switzerland
Tel.: (41-31) 350-3111
Fax: (41-31) 350-3110
E-mail: ib.info@ib.upu.org
Web site: www.upu.int
Director-General: Thomas E. Leavey
　　　　　(United States)

Founded in 1875 in Bern, the Universal Postal Union (UPU) became a UN specialized agency on July 1, 1948. Its role is to oversee the regulation of the international postal service, a truly universal system.

The UPU has 189 member states. Their postal services constitute the largest distribution network in the world. Each year, over 6 million postal workers in more than 700 000 post offices around the world handle a total of 430 billion letters, printed materials and packages in domestic postal services, and nearly 10 billion letters, printed materials and packages in the international postal service.

World Bank

1818 H Street NW
Washington, DC 20433, United States
Tel.: (202) 477-1234
Fax: (202) 477-6391
E-mail:
(firstname).(lastname)@worldbank.org
Web site: www.worldbank.org
President: James D. Wolfensohn
　　　　　(United States)

A product of the July 1944 Bretton Woods Agreement, the World Bank was set up to help with the postwar recovery of Europe; hence its official title, the International Bank for Reconstruction and Development (IBRD). When the role of the Bank in Europe was taken over by the Marshall Plan, its focus shifted to providing loans and technical help, especially in developing nations. The Bank's main role is to help raise living standards and promote sustainable development in developing countries.

Today, the World Bank Group comprises four bodies: the International Bank for Reconstruction and Development (IBRD), the International Finance Corporation (IFC), the International Development Association (IDA) and the Multilateral Investment Guarantee Agency (MIGA).

The Group offers loans, advice and a wide range of resources geared to the needs of over 100 developing countries or countries in transition. The Bank is the world's largest supplier of development aid, with some US$20 billion in new loans every year. The Bank also plays a vital co-ordinating role with a host of other organizations, governments, multilateral agencies and private firms: it ensures that the sums lent are used as efficiently as possible with a view to helping the recipient countries' development programs take shape.

Funds from loans are used to support a wide variety of projects in such fields as energy, agriculture, transportation, the environment, health care and education, with the general objective being to improve living standards in the recipient countries. The main goal is to make the world's poorest countries less poor. To that end, the Bank pays special attention to the development of rural regions and the role of women in development.

The Bank is funded by contributions from member states in the industrialized world and by borrowing in the commercial market. The Bank is owned by the 181 countries that make up both its borrowers and lenders. Canada is the eighth-biggest contributor to the World Bank, after the six other G-7 countries and Saudi Arabia.

World Health Organization

20, avenue Appia
CH-1211, Geneva 27, Switzerland
Tel.: (41-22) 791-3223/2584
Fax: (41-22) 791-4858
E-mail: info@who.int
Web site: www.who.org
Director-General: Gro Harlem Bruntland
(Norway)

Created in 1948, the 191-member World Health Organization (WHO) is at the forefront of the global alliance in support of health for all. A landmark victory came in 1980, when it was officially announced that smallpox had been eradicated. This disease had claimed millions of lives throughout the world before the international community, under WHO leadership, succeeded in wiping it out completely.

WHO's mandate is to promote international technical co-operation in support of global health, to develop and manage programs for controlling and eliminating disease and, in general, to work to improve the quality of life of people the world over.

The Organization's role is fourfold: *(a)* it provides world leadership in the field of health; *(b)* it sets world standards for health; *(c)* it co-operates with governments to strengthen national health programs; and *(d)* it develops and transfers appropriate technologies, information and health standards.

Recently, WHO reviewed and strengthened its global strategy in support of health for all by the year 2000. The goal is for people everywhere to have access to health services enabling them to lead socially and economically productive lives.

World Intellectual Property Organization

34, chemin des Colombettes
CH-1211, Geneva 20, Switzerland
Tel.: (41-22) 338-9111
Fax: (41-22) 733-5428
Telex: 412912
E-mail: publicinf@wipo.int
Web site: www.wipo.int
Director-General: Kamil Idris (Sudan)

The World Intellectual Property Organization (WIPO) was officially created in 1970 and became a UN specialized agency in 1974. However, its origins date back to 1893, with the founding of the United International Bureaux for the Protection of Intellectual Property. WIPO's mandate is to promote intellectual property protection around the world through co-operation between countries, and to ensure compliance with various multilateral treaties on legal and administrative aspects of intellectual property. WIPO has 171 member states.

Intellectual property covers two main areas:

* industrial property, including inventions, brand names, industrial designs and models, and labels of origin; and

* copyright, which applies chiefly to literary, musical, artistic, photographic and audiovisual works.

Basically, WIPO's role is to protect the livelihood of product creators by helping promote respect for their ideas, copyrights, patents and brand names around the world. In large part, its activities and resources are devoted to promoting development co-operation with developing countries.

World Meteorological Organization

41, avenue Giuseppe-Motta
CH 1211, Geneva 20, Switzerland
Tel.: (41-22) 730-8311
Fax: (41-22) 734-2326
Telex: 414199 OMM CH
E-mail: gorre.dale_e@gateway.wmo.ch
Web site: www.wmo.ch
Secretary-General: G.O.P. Obasi (Nigeria)

In 1951, the World Meteorological Organization (WMO) came into being and an agreement was signed conferring on it the status of UN specialized agency. With its 185 members—179 states and 6 territories—the WMO acts as the UN

system's scientific mouthpiece for all atmospheric and climatic issues affecting our planet.

WMO's mission is to facilitate global co-operation in meteorological observation and services, to promote expeditious exchanges of meteorological information and standardization in meteorological observations, and to ensure publication of observation data and corresponding statistics.

From weather forecasts to air pollution research, from studies of climate changes and the thinning of the ozone layer to forecasting tropical storms, WMO co-ordinates international scientific activities that help provide, more and more quickly, meteorological information and various services of constantly improving quality.

World Trade Organization

Centre William Rappard
154, rue de Lausanne
CH-1211, Geneva 21, Switzerland
Tel.: (41-22) 739-5111
Fax: (41-22) 731-4206
Telex: 412324 OMC/WTO CH
Web site: www.wto.org
Director-General: Mike Moore
(New Zealand)

The World Trade Organization (WTO) is an independent body with co-operative links to the United Nations. On January 1, 1995, it replaced the GATT, the third major international institution that grew out of the Bretton Woods Agreement. The WTO's main role is to promote free and non-discriminatory trade between nations. It has 133 member states, while 33 countries and 7 international organizations have WTO observer status.

From 1947 to December 31, 1994, the GATT was the forum for eight rounds of negotiations aimed at cutting tariffs throughout the world and helping international trade to expand. It was at the conclusion of the last of these, the Uruguay Round, that the World Trade Organization came into being.

The principal functions of the World Trade Organization are to administer trade agreements negotiated between member states, provide a framework for the negotiations, resolve trade disputes between member states, monitor national trade policies, provide developing countries with training and technical assistance, and co-operate with other international organizations to promote the harmonious expansion of trade around the world. Last, through the International Trade Centre, WTO provides special support for export promotion.

CIDA photo: Roger LeMoyne

Appendix

Appendix

The 188 Member States of the UN and their year of admission

1946	Afghanistan	1945	Chile
1955	Albania	1945	China
1962	Algeria	1945	Colombia
1993	Andorra	1975	Comoros
1976	Angola	1960	Congo
1981	Antigua and Barbuda	1945	Costa Rica
1945	Argentina	1960	Côte d'Ivoire
1992	Armenia	1992	Croatia
1945	Australia	1945	Cuba
1955	Austria	1960	Cyprus
1992	Azerbaijan	1993	Czech Republic[2]
1973	Bahamas	1991	Democratic People's Republic of Korea
1971	Bahrain		
1974	Bangladesh	1960	Democratic Republic of the Congo
1966	Barbados	1945	Denmark
1945	Belarus[1]	1977	Djibouti
1945	Belgium	1978	Dominica
1981	Belize	1945	Dominican Republic
1960	Benin	1945	Ecuador
1971	Bhutan	1945	Egypt[3]
1945	Bolivia	1945	El Salvador
1992	Bosnia and Herzegovina	1968	Equatorial Guinea
1966	Botswana	1993	Eritrea
1945	Brazil	1991	Estonia
1984	Brunei Darussalam	1945	Ethiopia
1955	Bulgaria	1970	Fiji
1960	Burkina Faso	1955	Finland
1962	Burundi	1945	France
1955	Cambodia	1960	Gabon
1960	Cameroon	1965	Gambia
1945	Canada	1992	Georgia
1975	Cape Verde	1973	Germany[4]
1960	Central African Republic	1957	Ghana
1960	Chad	1945	Greece

1974	Grenada	1961	Mongolia
1945	Guatemala	1956	Morocco
1958	Guinea	1975	Mozambique
1974	Guinea-Bissau	1948	Myanmar
1966	Guyana	1990	Namibia
1945	Haiti	1999	Nauru
1945	Honduras	1955	Nepal
1955	Hungary	1945	Netherlands
1946	Iceland	1945	New Zealand
1945	India	1945	Nicaragua
1950	Indonesia[5]	1960	Niger
1945	Iran (Islamic Republic of)	1960	Nigeria
1945	Iraq	1945	Norway
1955	Ireland	1971	Oman
1949	Israel	1947	Pakistan
1955	Italy	1994	Palau
1962	Jamaica	1945	Panama
1956	Japan	1975	Papua New Guinea
1955	Jordan	1945	Paraguay
1992	Kazakhstan	1945	Peru
1963	Kenya	1945	Philippines
1999	Kiribati	1945	Poland
1963	Kuwait	1955	Portugal
1992	Kyrgyzstan	1971	Qatar
1955	Lao People's Democratic Republic	1991	Republic of Korea
1991	Latvia	1992	Republic of Moldova
1945	Lebanon	1955	Romania
1966	Lesotho	1945	Russian Federation[7]
1945	Liberia	1962	Rwanda
1955	Libyan Arab Jamahiriya	1983	Saint Kitts and Nevis
1990	Liechtenstein	1979	Saint Lucia
1991	Lithuania	1980	Saint Vincent and the Grenadines
1945	Luxembourg	1976	Samoa
1960	Madagascar	1992	San Marino
1964	Malawi	1975	Sao Tome and Principe
1957	Malaysia[6]	1945	Saudi Arabia
1965	Maldives	1960	Senegal
1960	Mali	1976	Seychelles
1964	Malta	1961	Sierra Leone
1991	Marshall Islands	1965	Singapore
1961	Mauritania	1993	Slovakia[8]
1968	Mauritius	1992	Slovenia
1945	Mexico	1978	Solomon Islands
1991	Micronesia (Federated States of)	1960	Somalia
1993	Monaco	1945	South Africa

1955	Spain
1955	Sri Lanka
1956	Sudan
1975	Suriname
1968	Swaziland
1946	Sweden
1945	Syrian Arab Republic[9]
1992	Tajikistan
1946	Thailand
1993	The former Yugoslav Republic of Macedonia[10]
1960	Togo
1999	Tonga
1962	Trinidad and Tobago
1956	Tunisia
1945	Turkey
1992	Turkmenistan
1962	Uganda
1945	Ukraine
1971	United Arab Emirates
1945	United Kingdom of Great Britain and Northern Ireland
1961	United Republic of Tanzania[11]
1945	United States of America
1945	Uruguay
1992	Uzbekistan
1981	Vanuatu
1945	Venezuela
1977	Viet Nam
1947	Yemen[12]
1945	Yugoslavia
1964	Zambia
1980	Zimbabwe

Notes

1 On September 19, 1991, Byelorussia informed the United Nations that it had changed its name to Belarus.

2 Czechoslovakia was an original Member of the United Nations from October 24, 1945. In a letter dated December 10, 1992, its Permanent Representative informed the Secretary-General that the Czech and Slovak Federal Republic would cease to exist on December 31, 1992, and that the Czech Republic and the Slovak Republic, as successor States, would apply for membership in the United Nations. Following the receipt of its application, the Security Council, on January 8, 1993, recommended to the General Assembly that the Czech Republic be admitted to United Nations membership. The Czech Republic was thus admitted on January 19 as a Member State.

3 Egypt and Syria were original Members of the United Nations from October 24, 1945. Following a plebiscite on February 21, 1958, the United Arab Republic was established by a union of Egypt and Syria and continued as a single Member. On October 13, 1961, Syria, having resumed its status as an independent State, resumed its separate membership in the United Nations. On September 2, 1971, the United Arab Republic changed its name to the Arab Republic of Egypt.

4 The Federal Republic of Germany and the German Democratic Republic were admitted to membership in the United Nations on September 18, 1973. Through the accession of the German Democratic Republic to the Federal Republic of Germany, effective from October 3, 1990, the two German States have united to form one sovereign State.

5 By letter of January 20, 1965, Indonesia announced its decision to withdraw from the United Nations "at this stage and under the present circumstances." By telegram of September 19, 1966, it announced its decision "to resume full co-operation

with the United Nations and to resume participation in its activities." On September 28, 1966, the General Assembly took note of this decision and the President invited representatives of Indonesia to take seats in the Assembly.

6   The Federation of Malaya joined the United Nations on September 17, 1957. On September 16, 1963, its name was changed to Malaysia, following the admission to the new federation of Singapore, Sabah (North Borneo) and Sarawak. Singapore became an independent State on August 9, 1965, and a Member of the United Nations on September 21, 1965.

7   The Union of Soviet Socialist Republics was an original Member of the United Nations from October 24, 1945. In a letter dated December 24, 1991, Boris Yeltsin, the President of the Russian Federation, informed the Secretary-General that the membership of the Soviet Union in the Security Council and all other United Nations organs was being continued by the Russian Federation with the support of the 11 member countries of the Commonwealth of Independent States.

8   Czechoslovakia was an original Member of the United Nations from October 24, 1945. In a letter dated December 10, 1992, its Permanent Representative informed the Secretary-General that the Czech and Slovak Federal Republic would cease to exist on December 31, 1992, and that the Czech Republic and the Slovak Republic, as successor States, would apply for membership in the United Nations. Following the receipt of its application, the Security Council, on January 8, 1993, recommended to the General Assembly that the Slovak Republic be admitted to United Nations membership. The Slovak Republic was thus admitted on January 19 as a Member State.

9   Egypt and Syria were original Members of the United Nations from October 24, 1945. Following a plebiscite on February 21, 1958, the United Arab Republic was established by a union of Egypt and Syria and continued as a single Member. On October 13, 1961, Syria, having resumed its status as an independent State, resumed its separate membership in the United Nations.

10 The General Assembly decided on April 8, 1993, to admit to United Nations membership the State being provisionally referred to for all purposes within the United Nations as "The former Yugoslav Republic of Macedonia" pending settlement of the difference that had arisen over its name.

11 Tanganyika was a Member of the United Nations from December 14, 1961, and Zanzibar was a Member from December 16, 1963. Following the ratification on April 26, 1964, of Articles of Union between Tanganyika and Zanzibar, the United Republic of Tanganyika and Zanzibar continued as a single Member, changing its name to the United Republic of Tanzania on November 1, 1964.

12 Yemen was admitted to membership in the United Nations on September 30, 1947, and Democratic Yemen on December 14, 1967. On May 22, 1990, the two countries merged and have since been represented as one Member with the name "Yemen."

The United Nations on the Internet

•A•

- Administrative Committee on Co-ordination, Subcommittee on Nutrition (ACC/SCN) **www.unsystem.org/accscn/index.html**

•E•

- Economic Commission for Africa (ECA) **www.un.org/Depts/eca**
- Economic Commission for Europe (ECE) **www.unece.org**
- Economic Commission for Latin America and the Caribbean (ECLAC) **www.eclac.org**
- Economic and Social Commission for Asia and the Pacific (ESCAP) **www.unescap.org**

•F•

- Food and Agriculture Organization of the United Nations (FAO) **www.fao.org**

•I•

- Information Systems Co-ordination Committee (ISCC) **www.unsystem.org/iscc.html**
- International Atomic Energy Agency (IAEA) **www.iaea.int**
- International Bureau of Education (IBE) **www.ibe.unesco.org**
- International Civil Aviation Organization (ICAO) **www.icao.int**
- International Computing Centre (ICC) **www.unicc.org**
- International Court of Justice (ICJ) **www.icj-cij.org**
- International Fund for Agricultural Development (IFAD) **www.ifad.org**
- International Labour Organization (ILO) **www.ilo.org**
- International Maritime Organization (IMO) **www.imo.org**

- International Monetary Fund (IMF) **www.imf.org**
- International Research and Training Institute for the Advancement of Women (INSTRAW) **www.un.org/instraw**
- International Telecommunications Union (ITU) **www.itu.int**
- International Trade Centre (ITC) **www.intracen.org**

•J•

- Joint Inter-Agency Meeting on Computer-Assisted Translation and Terminology (JIAMCATT) **www.unsystem.org/jiamcatt**
- Joint United Nations Programme on HIV/AIDS (UNAIDS) **www.unaids.org**

•M•

- Multilateral Investment Guarantee Agency (MIGA) **www.miga.org**

•O•

- Outer Space Affairs, Office for (OOSA) **www.un.or.at/OOSA**

•U•

- United Nations Centre for Human Settlements / UNCHS (Habitat) **www.unchs.org**
- United Nations Children's Fund (UNICEF) **www.unicef.org**
- United Nations Conference on Trade and Development (UNCTAD) **www.unctad.org**
- United Nations Convention to Combat Desertification (UNCCD) **www.unccd.ch**
- United Nations Development Fund for Women (UNIFEM) **www.unifem.undp.org**

- United Nations Development Programme (UNDP) **www.undp.org**
- United Nations Educational, Scientific and Cultural Organization (UNESCO) **www.unesco.org**
- United Nations Environment Programme (UNEP) **www.unep.org**
- United Nations Framework Convention on Climate Change (UNFCCC) **www.unfccc.org**
- United Nations Headquarters (UN) **www.un.org**
- United Nations High Commissioner for Human Rights, Office of the (UNHCHR) **www.unhchr.ch**
- United Nations High Commissioner for Refugees, Office of the (UNHCR) **www.unhcr.ch**
- United Nations Industrial Development Organization (UNIDO) **www.unido.org**
- United Nations Institute for Disarmament Research (UNIDIR) **www.unog.ch/unidir**
- United Nations Institute for Training and Research (UNITAR) **www.unitar.org**
- United Nations International Drug Control Programme (UNDCP) **www.undcp.org**
- United Nations Interregional Crime and Justice Research Institute (UNICRI) **www.unicri.it**
- United Nations Office at Geneva (UNOG) **www.unog.ch**
- United Nations Office at Vienna (UNOV) **www.un.or.at**
- United Nations Office for Drug Control and Crime Prevention (ODCCP) **www.odccp.org**
- United Nations Office for Project Services (UNOPS) **www.unops.org**
- United Nations Population Fund (UNFPA) **www.unfpa.org**

- United Nations Research Institute for Social Development (UNRISD) **www.unrisd.org**
- United Nations University (UNU) **www.unu.edu**
- United Nations Volunteers (UNV) **www.unv.org**
- Universal Postal Union (UPU) **www.upu.int**

•W•

- World Bank (IBRD) **www.worldbank.org**
- World Food Programme (WFP) **www.wfp.org**
- World Health Organization (WHO) **www.who.org**
- World Intellectual Property Organization (WIPO) **www.wipo.int**
- World Meteorological Organization (WMO) **www.wmo.ch**
- World Tourism Organization **www.world-tourism.org**
- World Trade Organization (WTO) **www.wto.org**

Universal Declaration of Human Rights

 *Preamble*

Whereas recognition of the inherent dignity and of the equal and inalienable rights of all members of the human family is the foundation of freedom, justice and peace in the world,

Whereas disregard and contempt for human rights have resulted in barbarous acts which have outraged the conscience of mankind, and the advent of a world in which human beings shall enjoy freedom of speech and belief and freedom from fear and want has been proclaimed as the highest aspiration of the common people,

Whereas it is essential, if man is not to be compelled to have recourse, as a last resort, to rebellion against tyranny and oppression, that human rights should be protected by the rule of law,

Whereas it is essential to promote the development of friendly relations between nations,

Whereas the peoples of the United Nations have in the Charter re-affirmed their faith in fundamental human rights, in the dignity and worth of the human person and in the equal rights of men and women and have determined to promote social progress and better standards of life in larger freedom,

Whereas Member States have pledged themselves to achieve, in co-operation with the United Nations, the promotion of universal respect for and observance of human rights and fundamental freedoms,

Whereas a common understanding of these rights and freedoms is of the greatest importance for the full realization of this pledge,

Now, Therefore the General Assembly proclaims this Universal Declaration of Human Rights as a common standard of achievement for all peoples and all nations, to the end that every individual and every organ of society, keeping this Declaration constantly in mind, shall strive by teaching and education to promote respect for these rights and freedoms and by progressive measures, national and international, to secure their universal and effective recognition and observance, both among the peoples of Member States themselves and among the peoples of territories under their jurisdiction.

Article 1

All human beings are born free and equal in dignity and rights. They are endowed with reason and conscience and should act towards one another in a spirit of brotherhood.

Article 2

1   Everyone is entitled to all the rights and freedoms set forth in this Declaration, without distinction of any kind, such as race, colour, sex, language, religion, political or other opinion, national or social origin, property, birth or other status.

2   Furthermore, no distinction shall be made on the basis of the political, jurisdictional or international status of the country or territory to which a person belongs, whether it be independent, trust, non-self-governing or under any other limitation of sovereignty.

Article 3

Everyone has the right to life, liberty and security of person.

Article 4

No one shall be held in slavery or servitude; slavery and the slave trade shall be prohibited in all their forms.

Article 5

No one shall be subjected to torture or to cruel, inhuman or degrading treatment or punishment.

Article 6

Everyone has the right to recognition everywhere as a person before the law.

Article 7

All are equal before the law and are entitled without any discrimination to equal protection of the law. All are entitled to equal protection against any discrimination in violation of this Declaration and against any incitement to such discrimination.

Article 8

Everyone has the right to an effective remedy by the competent national tribunals for acts violating the fundamental rights granted him by the constitution or by law.

Article 9

No one shall be subjected to arbitrary arrest, detention or exile.

Article 10

Everyone is entitled in full equality to a fair and public hearing by an independent and impartial tribunal, in the determination of his rights and obligations and of any criminal charge against him.

Article 11

1   Everyone charged with a penal offence has the right to be presumed innocent until proved guilty according to law in a public trial at which he has had all the guarantees necessary for his defence.

2   No one shall be held guilty of any penal offence on account of any act or omission which did not constitute a penal offence, under national or international law, at the time when it was committed. Nor shall a heavier penalty be imposed than the one that was applicable at the time the penal offence was committed.

Article 12

No one shall be subjected to arbitrary interference with his privacy, family, home or correspondence, nor to attacks upon his honour and reputation. Everyone has the right to the protection of the law against such interference or attacks.

Article 13

1   Everyone has the right to freedom of movement and residence within the borders of each state.

2   Everyone has the right to leave any country, including his own, and to return to his country.

Article 14

1   Everyone has the right to seek and to enjoy in other countries asylum from persecution.

2   This right may not be invoked in the case of prosecutions genuinely arising from non-political crimes or from acts contrary to the purposes and principles of the United Nations.

Article 15

1   Everyone has the right to a nationality.

2   No one shall be arbitrarily deprived of his nationality nor denied the right to change his nationality.

Article 16

1   Men and women of full age, without any limitation due to race, nationality or religion, have the right to marry and to found a family. They are entitled to equal rights as to marriage, during marriage and at its dissolution.

2   Marriage shall be entered into only with the free and full consent of the intending spouses.

3   The family is the natural and fundamental group unit of society and is entitled to protection by society and the State.

Article 17

1   Everyone has the right to own property alone as well as in association with others.

2   No one shall be arbitrarily deprived of his property.

Article 18

Everyone has the right to freedom of thought, conscience and religion; this right includes freedom to change his religion or belief, and freedom, either alone or in community with others and in public or private, to manifest his religion or belief in teaching, practice, worship and observance.

Article 19

Everyone has the right to freedom of opinion and expression; this right includes freedom to hold opinions without interference and to seek, receive and impart information and ideas through any media and regardless of frontiers.

Article 20

1   Everyone has the right to freedom of peaceful assembly and association.

2   No one may be compelled to belong to an association.

Article 21

1   Everyone has the right to take part in the government of his country, directly or through freely chosen representatives.

2   Everyone has the right of equal access to public service in his country.

3   The will of the people shall be the basis of the authority of government; this will shall be expressed in periodic and genuine elections which shall be by universal and equal suffrage and shall be held by secret vote or by equivalent free voting procedures.

Article 22

Everyone, as a member of society, has the right to social security and is entitled to realization, through national effort and international co-operation and in accordance with the organization and resources of each State, of the economic, social and cultural rights indispensable for his dignity and the free development of his personality.

Article 23

1   Everyone has the right to work, to free choice of employment, to just and favourable conditions of work and to protection against unemployment.

2   Everyone, without any discrimination, has the right to equal pay for equal work.

3   Everyone who works has the right to just and favourable remuneration ensuring for himself and his family an existence worthy of human dignity, and supplemented, if necessary, by other means of social protection.

4   Everyone has the right to form and to join trade unions for the protection of his interests.

Article 24

Everyone has the right to rest and leisure, including reasonable limitation of working hours and periodic holidays with pay.

Article 25

1   Everyone has the right to a standard of living adequate for the health and well-being of himself and of his family, including food, clothing, housing and medical care and necessary social services, and the right to security in the event of unemployment, sickness, disability, widowhood, old age or other lack of livelihood in circumstances beyond his control.

2   Motherhood and childhood are entitled to special care and assistance. All children, whether born in or out of wedlock, shall enjoy the same social protection.

Article 26

1   Everyone has the right to education. Education shall be free, at least in the elementary and fundamental stages. Elementary education shall be compulsory. Technical and professional education shall be made generally available and higher education shall be equally accessible to all on the basis of merit.

2   Education shall be directed to the full development of the human personality and to the strengthening of respect for human rights and fundamental freedoms. It shall promote understanding, tolerance and friendship among all nations, racial or religious groups, and shall further the activities of the United Nations for the maintenance of peace.

3   Parents have a prior right to choose the kind of education that shall be given to their children.

Article 27

1   Everyone has the right freely to participate in the cultural life of the community, to enjoy the arts and to share in scientific advancement and its benefits.

2   Everyone has the right to the protection of the moral and material interests resulting from any scientific, literary or artistic production of which he is the author.

Article 28

Everyone is entitled to a social and international order in which the rights and freedoms set forth in this Declaration can be fully realized.

Article 29

1   Everyone has duties to the community in which alone the free and full development of his personality is possible.

2   In the exercise of his rights and freedoms, everyone shall be subject only to such limitations as are determined by law solely for the purpose of securing due recognition and respect for the rights and freedoms of others and of meeting the just requirements of morality, public order and the general welfare in a democratic society.

3   These rights and freedoms may in no case be exercised contrary to the purposes and principles of the United Nations.

Article 30

Nothing in this Declaration may be interpreted as implying for any State, group or person any right to engage in any activity or to perform any act aimed at the destruction of any of the rights and freedoms set forth herein.

Days, Weeks, Years and Decades proclaimed by the United Nations

UN Days

March 8
International Women's Day

March 21
International Day for the Elimination of
Racial Discrimination

March 22
World Day for Water

March 23
World Meteorological Day

April 7
World Health Day

May 3
International Day of Families

May 17
World Telecommunications Day

May 31
World No-Tobacco Day

June 4
International Day of Innocent Children
Victims of Aggression

June 5
World Environment Day

June 26
International Day against Drug Abuse
and Illicit Trafficking

July 11
World Population Day

September 8
International Literacy Day

October 1
International Day of Older Persons

October 9
World Post Day

October 16
World Food Day

October 17
International Day for the
Eradication of Poverty

October 24
United Nations Day

October 24
World Development Information Day

November 16
International Day for Tolerance

November 20
Universal Children's Day
(date varies from year to year)

November 20
Africa Industrialization Day

November 29
International Day of Solidarity
with the Palestinian People

December 1
World AIDS Day

December 3
International Day of Disabled Persons

December 5
International Volunteer Day for
Economic and Social Development

December 10
Human Rights Day

Other Days

third Tuesday in September
International Day of Peace (opening day of the regular annual session of the General Assembly**)**

during last week of September
World Maritime Day

first Monday in October
World Habitat Day

second Wednesday in October
International Day for Natural Disaster Reduction

UN Weeks

March 21–28
Week of Solidarity with the Peoples Struggling against Racism and Racial Discrimination

October 24–30
Disarmament Week

week of November 11
International Week of Science and Peace

UN Years

1999
International Year of Older Persons

2000
International Year for the Culture of Peace

2000
International Year of Thanksgiving

2001
International Year of Volunteers

UN Decades

1990–99
United Nations Decade of International Law

1990–2000
Fourth Transport and Communications Decade in Africa

1990–2000
International Decade for Natural Disaster Reduction

1990–2000
Third Disarmament Decade

1991–2000
United Nations Decade against Drug Abuse

1993–2002
Second Industrial Development Decade for Africa

1993–2002
Asian and Pacific Decade of Disabled Persons

1993–2003
Third Decade to Combat Racism and Racial Discrimination

1995–2004
International Decade of the World's Indigenous People

Secretary-General
Kofi Annan

UN/DPI photo: Milton Grant

The seventh Secretary-General of the United Nations, Kofi Annan is, of all those who have held the position, the one with the most experience in the organization. When appointed in December 1996 for a five-year term commencing in January 1997, Mr. Annan, who has spent more than 30 years at the UN, was Under-Secretary-General for Peacekeeping Operations.

Born on April 8, 1938, at Kumasi, Ghana, Mr. Annan is fluent in English, French and several African languages. After studying at the University of Sciences and Technologies in Kumasi, he received a degree in economics from Macalester College in St. Paul, Minnesota, in 1961. After a year at the Institut universitaire des hautes études internationales in Geneva, he began working for the

World Health Organization. A few years later, he went back to school and in 1972 obtained a master's degree in management from the Massachusetts Institute of Technology before joining the UN.

Mr. Annan has performed a wide range of duties in his career at the UN, becoming involved not only in management—administration, budgets, finance and personnel—but also in refugee problems and peacekeeping matters. He distinguished himself by leading a number of delicate diplomatic missions, including the negotiations to repatriate over 900 international civil servants and to liberate Western hostages in Iraq following that country's invasion of Kuwait in 1990, the development of the "oil for food" formula adopted in response to the humanitarian crisis in Iraq, and the supervision of the transition phase between the United Nations Protection Force (UNPROFOR) in the former Yugoslavia and NATO's Implementation Force (IFOR) following the signing of the Dayton peace accord in 1995.

Deputy Secretary-General
Louise Fréchette

UN/DPI photo: Milton Grant

Born in Montréal on July 16, 1946, Louise Fréchette was appointed to the post of Deputy Secretary-General of the United Nations at the end of February 1998, following the adoption by the General Assembly of the program of reforms proposed by Mr. Annan. Ms. Fréchette has had a long career in diplomacy, having held several important positions in Canada's Department of Foreign Affairs and International Trade, which she joined in 1971.

Among her many positions, she served as Canada's Ambassador to Argentina and Uruguay, Assistant Deputy Minister for Latin America and the Caribbean, and Assistant Deputy Minister for Economic Policy and Trade Competitiveness. In 1994, Ms. Fréchette was Canada's Ambassador to the United Nations in New York before being appointed in June 1995 as Canada's Deputy Minister of National Defence. She graduated from the Université de Montréal with a degree in history, and from the College of Europe in Bruges with a diploma in economic studies.

*For complete biographies of Mr. Annan and Ms. Fréchette, visit the United Nations Web site at **www.un.org**.*

Past Secretaries-General

UN photo 178980: Milton Grant.

Boutros Boutros-Ghali
(Egypt)
January 1, 1992, to December 31, 1996

Born in Cairo on November 14, 1922, Boutros Boutros-Ghali is a lawyer and a career diplomat. After receiving a doctorate in international law from the Université de Paris in 1949, he taught international law and international relations at the University of Cairo until his appointment as Egypt's Minister of State for Foreign Affairs in 1977.

Heavily involved in international affairs, he had a hand in negotiating the Camp David accords signed by Egypt and Israel in 1979. He headed the Egyptian delegation to the UN General Assembly in 1979, 1982 and 1990. Before taking up his duties as UN Secretary-General on January 1, 1992, he also served as Vice-President of the Socialist International.

UN photo 169681

Javier Pérez de Cuéllar
(Peru)
January 1, 1982, to December 31, 1991

Javier Pérez de Cuéllar was born in Lima on January 19, 1920. He joined the Peruvian Ministry of Foreign Affairs in 1940 and eventually made his way to the top, serving as Ambassador to Switzerland, the Soviet Union, Poland and Venezuela. In 1971 he was named Peru's Permanent Representative to the United Nations.

In 1973 and 1974 he represented his country on the Security Council, serving as President of the Council during the Cyprus crisis in July 1974. On September 18, 1975, he was named Special Representative of the Secretary-General in Cyprus, a post he held until December 1977. In 1979 he was appointed United Nations Under-Secretary-General for Special Political Affairs. In May 1981 he returned to Lima, where he remained until his appointment as UN Secretary-General in December of that year. He served two terms.

Kurt Waldheim
(Austria)
January 1, 1972, to December 31, 1981

UN photo 122690: Y. Nagata

Born in Sankt Andrä-Wörden, near Vienna, on December 21, 1918, Kurt Waldheim is a lawyer and career diplomat. After receiving a doctorate in law from the University of Vienna, he joined the diplomatic service in 1945 and was appointed the Permanent Observer for Austria to the United Nations in 1955, and then the head of the Austrian mission when Austria was admitted to the United Nations.

From 1956 to 1960, he represented Austria in Canada. He then returned to Vienna, where he served as Director-General for Political Affairs. In 1964, he was named Austria's Permanent Representative to the United Nations. From 1968 to 1970 he served as his country's Minister of Foreign Affairs before being re-appointed Austria's Representative to the UN. He held this post until he was named Secretary-General at the end of 1971. After his diplomatic career, he served as President of the Austrian Republic from 1986 to 1992.

U Thant
(Myanmar—formerly Burma)
November 3, 1961, to December 31, 1971

UN photo: Y. Nagata

Born at Pantanaw, Myanmar on January 22, 1909, U Thant worked in the field of education and for the government, where he served as Director of Broadcasting, before joining the diplomatic service. In the 1950s he worked in the Prime Minister's office and headed Burma's Economic and Social Board.

In the early 1960s, he represented his country at the UN. On November 3, 1961, he was appointed to fill the unexpired term of Dag Hammarskjöld, who had died in an air crash. One year later he was appointed for a term of office ending in November 1966, and was subsequently re-elected for another term ending December 31, 1971. U Thant had to deal with an unprecedented number of serious international crises requiring deft handling, including African decolonization, the Cuban missile crisis in 1962, the Indo-Pakistani crisis in 1965, the Middle East war in 1967 and the Vietnam war. U Thant was also a writer, authoring a number of books including *The League of Nations* in 1933. He died in New York in 1974.

UN photo 62336

Dag Hammarskjöld
(Sweden)
April 7, 1953, to September 1961

Born on July 29, 1905, in Jonkoping, Sweden, Dag Hammarskjöld met with a tragic fate when he died in a plane crash in Zambia in September 1961. After receiving a doctorate in law and political science, he taught at the University of Stockholm before becoming Under-Secretary of the Finance Ministry and then Chairman of the Board of the National Bank of Sweden from 1941 to 1948.

Dag Hammarskjöld joined the Foreign Office in 1946 as a financial adviser. In 1950 he was appointed Minister of State. Later, he led his country's delegation to the General Assembly and, on April 7, 1953, was appointed Secretary-General of the United Nations. He was unanimously re-elected for a second term on September 26, 1957. He was posthumously awarded the Nobel Peace Prize in 1961.

UN photo 22731

Trygve Halvdan Lie
(Norway)
February 1, 1946, to April 7, 1953

Trygve Lie was born in Oslo on July 16, 1896. He was elected a member of the Norwegian Parliament in 1935, and served as Minister of Justice, Minister of Trade, and Minister of Supply and Shipping. When his country was invaded by Germany, he fled with his government to London and in 1941 became Foreign Minister for the Norwegian government in exile.

In 1945 he led his country's delegation to the San Francisco Conference, where the UN Charter was signed. There he chaired the commission responsible for drafting the Security Council provisions of the Charter. The following year, he led the Norwegian delegation to the first session of the General Assembly, held in London. It was there that he was elected the first Secretary-General of the United Nations. On November 1, 1950, his term of office was extended by three years, but in 1952 he submitted his resignation. He died on December 30, 1968, at the age of 72.

*For complete biographies, visit the United Nations Web site at **www.un.org**.*

Canada's Representatives to the UN since 1948

Gen. Andrew McNaughton
January 1948 to December 1949

John W. Holmes
January to June 1950

R.G. Riddell
June 1950 to June 1951

David M. Johnson
November 1951 to August 1955

R. A. Mackay
August 1955 to November 1957

Charles S.A. Ritchie
January 1958 to February 1962

Pierre Tremblay
July 1962 to June 1966

George Ignatieff
July 1966 to February 1969

Yvon Beaulne
February 1969 to June 1972

Saul F. Rae
July 1972 to July 1976

William H. Barton
August 1976 to April 1980

Michel Dupuy
April 1980 to May 1981

Gérard Pelletier
May 1981 to August 1984

Stephen Lewis
August 1984 to August 1988

Yves Fortier
August 1988 to December 1991

Louise Fréchette
January 1992 to December 1994

Robert Fowler
from January 1995

CIDA photo: David Barbour

Canadians who served with distinction within the United Nations

Lt.-Gen. Maurice Baril
Senior military adviser to the Secretary-General in 1992; headed the Department of Peacekeeping Operations during the 1990s.

Alan Beesley
Central figure in the negotiations that led to the Law of the Sea Convention (1967–82). Proponent of the idea that the oceans belong to the "common heritage of mankind."

Harry Black
Served as Executive Director of UNICEF in the 1970s.

Lt.-Gen. E.L. Burns
Assembled and led the United Nations Emergency Force, which defused the Suez Crisis in 1956. Served as Chief of Staff for the United Nations Truce Supervision Organization.

James Carney
Helped launch an aid program for developing nations by producing over 200 films for the United Nations Conference on Human Settlements in 1976. Commissioner-General for the UN Pavilion at Expo 86 in Vancouver.

Margaret Catley-Carlson
Deputy Executive Director of Operations at UNICEF, with the rank of UN Under-Secretary-General (1981–83).

Brock Chisholm
First Director-General of the World Health Organization.

Rt. Hon. Joe Clark
Former Prime Minister and Secretary of State for External Affairs, served as Special Representative of the Secretary-General for Cyprus. Also played an important role in mobilizing international opinion against apartheid in South Africa.

Justice Jules Deschênes
Chaired the Commission of Inquiry on Romania (1989–91). Served as a consultant for the UN Centre for Social Development and Humanitarian Affairs in Vienna (1983–85). Judge on the international tribunals investigating war crimes committed in the former Yugoslavia and Rwanda.

Elizabeth Dowdeswell
Canada's Permanent Representative to the World Meteorological Organization. Executive Director of the UN Environment Programme in 1992. A world expert on climate.

William Epstein
Secretary of the United Nations Disarmament Commission (1952–72). Director of the Department for Disarmament Affairs (1954–72). Played an important role in numerous negotiating sessions leading to the signing of several arms control treaties, including the Partial Test Ban Treaty (1963) and the Biological Weapons Convention (1972).

Col. Don Ethell
Commanded the Canadian contingent serving under the United Nations Disengagement Observer

Force in the Middle East. Helped bring about large-scale prisoner of war exchanges between Syria and Israel. Called out of retirement to lead Canadian personnel taking part in the European Co-operation Commission's observer mission in the former Yugoslavia.

Ron Gould

Organized the UN mission to Nicaragua (1989). Led a fact-finding mission to Cambodia to help plan and organize the 1991 elections. Directed the UN's Electoral Assistance Division in Mozambique (1994) and took part in the UN's pre-electoral mission to Tanzania (1995).

John Peters Humphrey

Organized the Human Rights Division of the UN Secretariat. Wrote the first draft of the Universal Declaration of Human Rights and oversaw the debates on the Declaration in the General Assembly.

Paul Ignatieff

Worked for UNICEF throughout the world. Served as UNICEF representative in Japan, then as Director of its Geneva office.

Philippe Kirsch

Legal Adviser, Department of Foreign Affairs and International Trade. Deputy Ambassador to the UN (1988–92). Chaired the Special Working Group on Peacekeeping. Chaired the UN's Judicial Commission (1982) and the drafting committees of several international human rights conventions. In 1998, chaired the Committee of the Whole of the Conference on the Treaty of Rome establishing the International Criminal Court, a first in international human rights law.

Stephen Lewis

Canada's Ambassador to the United Nations (1984–88). Chaired the committee that designed the UN's five-year program for African economic recovery. Secretary-General's special adviser on Africa (1986–91). Deputy Director (external relations) for UNICEF in 1995. Member of the advisory group for the Fourth World Conference on Women (1995).

Maj.-Gen. Lewis MacKenzie

Participated in seven peace missions throughout the world. Chief of Staff of the United Nations Protection Force (UNPROFOR) in the former Yugoslavia in 1992.

Elisabeth Mann-Borgese

Expert on law of the sea. Received the UNEP Sasakawa Environment Prize in 1987.

Lucien Michaud

Chair of the Council of the United Nations University since 1995.

Tamar Oppenheimer

Secretary-General of the International Conference on Drug Abuse and Illicit Trafficking in 1987.

Thérèse Paquet-Sévigny

Under-Secretary-General of the UN's Information Department in 1987. Chair (Communications and International Development) of UNESCO.

Rt. Hon. Lester B. Pearson

Former Prime Minister and Secretary of State for External Affairs. Represented Canada at the San Francisco Conference in 1945. The only Canadian to serve as President of the General Assembly (1952–53). Developed the concept of peace-keeping, which brought a halt to the Suez Crisis in 1956, earning him the Nobel Peace Prize.

Escott Reid

Led Canada's delegation to the San Francisco Conference in 1945. Subsequently worked for a number of organizations, including the World Bank.

Douglas Roche

Canada's Ambassador for Disarmament to the United Nations (1984–89) and former chair of the First Committee (Peace and Security).

Maurice Strong

Former Secretary-General of the UN Conference on the Environment (1972), first Executive Director of UNEP, Co-ordinator of the UN's Office for Emergency Operations in Africa (1985–86), and Secretary-General of UNCTAD (1992). Also chaired the World Federation of United Nations Associations (WFUNA) and the 1992 Earth Summit in Rio.

Gerald Trant

Executive Director of the World Food Council in 1986.

Harry Winsor

Joined FAO in 1946. Organized the first regional fisheries development project in the West Indies. Was the first Director of Operations (Fisheries) at the FAO (1968–74), and FAO Senior Director (1974–79).

CIDA photo: David Barbour

Canadian Missions to the United Nations

Permanent Mission of Canada to the United Nations in New York
1 Dag Hammarskjöld Plaza
885 Second Avenue, 14th Floor, New York
NY 10017, USA
Tel.: (212) 848-1100
Fax: (212) 848-1195, 848-1192
E-mail: prmny@prmny01.x400.gc.ca
Permanent Representative, Ambassador:
Robert R. Fowler

Permanent Mission of Canada to the Office of the United Nations at Geneva, to the Conference on Disarmament, and to the World Trade Organization
1, rue du Pré-de-la-Bichett
1202 Geneva, Switzerland
Tel.: (41-22) 919-9200
Fax (general): (41-22) 919-9233
Administration / Consular Affairs:
(41-22) 919-9271
Humanitarian Affairs: (41-22) 919-9295
Trade (WTO): (41-22) 919-9290
United Nations / Disarmament:
(41-22) 919-9227
E-mail: genev@dfait-maeci.gc.ca
Permanent Representative, Ambassador
to the Office of the United Nations and
to the World Trade Organization:
Sergio Marchi

Permanent Mission of Canada to the International Organizations in Vienna: United Nations Office at Vienna, United Nations Industrial Development Organization, International Atomic Energy Agency
Laurenzerberg 2, A-1010 Vienna, Austria
Tel.: (43-1) 531-383001
Fax: (43-1) 531-383903
Telex: 115320
E-mail: vperm@vienn01.x400.gc.ca
Ambassador and Permanent
Representative: Paul Dubois

Permanent Mission of Canada to the Food and Agriculture Organization
30, Via Zara, 00198 Rome, Italy
Tel.: (39-06) 445-98551
Fax: (39-06) 445-98930
Permanent Representative:
Jeremy K.B. Kinsman

Permanent Mission of Canada to the International Civil Aviation Organization
999 University Street, Suite 15.35
Montréal, Quebec H3C 5J9
Tel.: (514) 954-5800
Fax: (514) 954-5809
Representative: Ghislaine Richard

Permanent Mission of Canada to the United Nations Centre for Human Settlements and Permanent Mission of Canada to the United Nations Environment Programme
Comcraft House, Haile Selassie Avenue
P.O. Box 30481, Nairobi, Kenya
Tel.: (254-2) 214-804
Fax: (254-2) 216-485
Permanent Representative:
Gerry Campbell

Permanent Delegation of Canada to the United Nations Educational, Scientific and Cultural Organization
1, rue Miollis, 75015 Paris, France
Tel.: (33-1) 456-83517
Fax: (33-1) 430-68727
Telex: 280806
E-mail: pesco@paris03.x400.gc.ca
Ambassador and Permanent Delegate:
Jacques Demers

UN and UN-related offices in Canada

Canadian Commission for UNESCO
350 Albert Street, P.O. Box 1047
Ottawa, Ontario K1P 5V8
Tel.: (613) 566-4414, ext. 4558
Fax: (613) 566-4405
E-mail:
louis.patenaude@conseildesarts.ca
Acting Secretary-General:
Louis Patenaude

Canadian Commission for UNIFEM
250 Albert Street, Suite 546
Ottawa, Ontario K1G 3H9
Tel.: (613) 236-6163 ext. 2119
Web site: www.unifem.ca
President: Aldea Landry

**Canadian Society for International
Health (linked to WHO and Pan
American Health Organization)**
1 Nicholas Street, Suite 1105
Ottawa, Ontario K1N 7B7
Tel.: (613) 241-5785
Fax: (613) 241-3845
E-mail: csih@fox.nstn.ca
Executive Director: Charles Shields

International Atomic Energy Agency
365 Bloor Street East, Suite 1702
Toronto, Ontario M4W 3L4
Tel.: (416) 928-9149
Fax: (416) 928-0046
Head: M.G. Madueme

**International Civil Aviation
Organization**
999 University Street
Montréal, Quebec H3C 5H7
Tel.: (514) 954-8221
Fax: (514) 954-6077
Secretary-General: R.C. Costa Pereira

**Secretariat for the Convention on
Biological Diversity**
World Trade Centre
413 Saint-Jacques Street, Suite 6310
Montréal, Quebec
H2Y 1N9
Tel.: (514) 288-2220
Fax: (514) 288-6588
E-mail: biodiv@mtl.net
Executive Secretary: Calestous Juma

United Nations Association in Canada
130 Slater Street, Suite 900
Ottawa, Ontario K1P 6E2
Tel.: (613) 232-5751
Fax: (613) 563-2455
E-mail: unac@magi.com
Web site: www.unac.org
Executive Director: Harry Qualman
National President: Muriel Smith

**United Nations Children's Fund
(UNICEF Canada)**
443 Mount Pleasant Road
Toronto, Ontario M4S 2L8
Tel.: (416) 482-4444
Fax: (416) 482-8035
E-mail: secretary@unicef.ca
Web site: www.unicef.ca
Executive Director: Harry Black

Ottawa UNICEF office:
379 Bank Street
Ottawa, Ontario K2P 1Y3
Tel.: (613) 233-8842
Fax: (613) 235-3522

United Nations Educational, Scientific and Cultural Organization (UNESCO) Liaison Office for Canada
56 Saint-Pierre Street, Suite 1550
Québec, Quebec G1K 4A1
Tel.: (418) 692-3333
Fax: (418) 692-2562
E-mail: unesco.quebec@unesco.org
Director: Ndèye Fall

United Nations Environment Programme Multilateral Fund
1800 McGill College Avenue
Montreal Trust Building, 27th Floor
Montréal, Quebec H3A 3J6
Tel.: (514) 282-1122
Fax: (514) 282-0068
Head: Omar El Arini

United Nations High Commissioner for Refugees
280 Albert Street, Suite 401
Ottawa, Ontario K1P 5G8
Tel.: (613) 232-0909
Fax: (613) 230-1855
E-mail: canot@unhcr.ch
Representative of the High
Commissioner: Yilma Makonnen

World University Service of Canada (Canadian contact for UN Volunteers)
1404 Scott Street
P.O. Box 3000, Station C
Ottawa, Ontario K1Y 4M8
Tel.: (613) 798-7477
Fax: (613) 798-0990
E-mail: loraine@wusc.ca
Web site: www.wusc.ca
Program Officer: Loraine Piquette

United Nations Association in Canada

As a large-scale international organization, the United Nations may seem very distant and inaccessible to the general public. Although it is not a world government, it faces a challenge familiar to democratic governments: staying in touch with its constituents.

To narrow the gap between the UN and ordinary citizens, over the years a network of voluntary UN associations has grown up in 80 countries.

One of the most active is the United Nations Association in Canada (UNA-Canada). From its small national headquarters in Ottawa and 15 branches across the country, the 15 000-member organization works year-round to promote Canadian understanding of the UN and support for its cause.

The essence of the task is communication. UNA-Canada is a national clearing house for information about the UN. Among other things, it fields public and media inquiries, publishes a newsletter and other material, and operates a Web site. It also keeps Canadian industry up to date on UN-related business opportunities.

Locally and nationally, the Association is a tireless proponent of international co-operation, marshalling public and government support for UN action on such issues as landmines, human rights, food security, and the financial crisis caused by non-payment of UN dues on the part of some members.

The national office organizes annual events, including gala dinners that combine fund-raising with promotion by featuring UN officials as keynote speakers. Each year, the Association awards the Pearson Peace Medal for distinguished service in support of human rights and other international causes.

With the UN turning 54 years old in 1999, UNA-Canada is focussing special attention on youth. Says Executive Director Harry Qualman, "People who can remember when and why the UN came into being are gradually passing from the scene. We have to guard against a generation gap in understanding."

UNA-Canada's youth programs include the following:

* support, through its branches, for model UN Assemblies in which high school and university students take the part of member states in the General Assembly and the Security Council;

* operation of an internship program funded by the Department of Foreign Affairs and International Trade, which places recent university graduates in UN and UN-related offices abroad; and

* a regular poll of Canadians about their UN views. ("Support has stayed high over the years," says Mr. Qualman. "We take some credit for that.")

For more information, contact:

UN Association in Canada
130 Slater Street, Suite 900
Ottawa, Ontario K1P 6E2
Tel.: (613) 232-5751
Fax: (613) 563-2455
E-mail: unac@magi.com or info@unac.org
Web site: www.unac.org

Individual Canadians can become involved in UNA-Canada by joining the Association, attending or organizing UN-related public events in their community, or making their views about the UN known to their elected representatives

United Nations system acronyms

ACC	Administrative Co-ordination Committee		**ICSC**	International Civil Service Commission
ECA	Economic Commission for Africa		**IFAD**	International Fund for Agricultural Development
ECE	Economic Commission for Europe		**ILO**	International Labour Organization
ECLAC	Economic Commission for Latin America and the Caribbean		**IMF**	International Monetary Fund
ECOSOC	Economic and Social Council		**IMO**	International Maritime Organization
ESCAP	Economic and Social Commission for Asia and the Pacific		**INSTRAW**	International Research and Training Institute for the Advancement of Women
ESCWA	Economic and Social Commission for Western Asia		**ISCC**	Information Systems Consultative Committee
FAO	Food and Agriculture Organization		**ITC**	International Trade Centre
FCCC	Framework Convention on Climate Change		**ITU**	International Telecommunications Union
IAEA	International Atomic Energy Agency		**MIGA**	Multilateral Investment Guarantee Agency
IBE	International Bureau of Education		**OHCHR**	Office of the United Nations High Commissioner for Human Rights
IBRD	International Bank for Reconstruction and Development (World Bank)		**UN**	United Nations
ICAO	International Civil Aviation Organization		**UNCHS (Habitat)**	United Nations Centre for Human Settlements
ICC	International Computing Centre		**UNCIVPOL**	United Nations Civilian Police
ICJ	International Court of Justice		**UNCTAD**	United Nations Conference on Trade and Development
			UNDCP	United Nations International Drug Control Programme

UNDP	United Nations Development Programme	**UNON**	United Nations Office at Nairobi
UNEP	United Nations Environment Programme	**UNOPS**	United Nations Office for Project Services
UNESCO	United Nations Educational, Scientific and Cultural Organization	**UNOV**	United Nations Office at Vienna
UNFPA	United Nations Population Fund	**UNRISD**	United Nations Research Institute for Social Development
UNGA	United Nations General Assembly	**UNRWA**	United Nations Relief and Works Agency for Palestine Refugees in the Near East
UNHCHR	United Nations High Commissioner for Human Rights	**UNSC**	United Nations Security Council
UNHCR	(Office of the) United Nations High Commissioner for Refugees	**UNU**	United Nations University
UNICEF	United Nations Children's Fund	**UNV**	United Nations Volunteers
		UPU	Universal Postal Union
UNICRI	United Nations Interregional Crime and Justice Research Institute	**WFP**	World Food Programme
		WHO	World Health Organization
UNIDIR	United Nations Institute for Disarmament Research	**WIPO**	World Intellectual Property Organization
UNIDO	United Nations Industrial Development Organization	**WMO**	World Meteorological Organization
UNIFEM	United Nations Development Fund for Women	**WTO**	World Trade Organization
UNITAR	United Nations Institute for Training and Research		
UNOG	United Nations Office at Geneva		

Select bibliography

Allan, James H. *Peacekeeping: Outspoken Observations by a Field Officer.* Westport, Conn.: Praeger, 1996.

Allsebrook, Mary. *Prototypes of Peacemaking: The First Forty Years of the United Nations.* Chicago: St. James Press, 1986.

Amer, Ramses. *The United Nations and Foreign Military Interventions: A Comparative Study of the Application of the Charter.* Uppsala, Sweden: Uppsala University, Department of Peace and Conflict Research; Philadelphia, Penn.: Coronet Books, 1992.

Arend, Anthony C., and Robert J. Beck. *International Law and the Use of Force: Beyond the UN Charter Paradigm.* London and New York: Routledge, 1993.

Baehr, Peter R., and Leon Gordenker. *The United Nations: Reality and Ideal.* New York: Praeger; 1984.

————. *The United Nations in the 1990s.* 2nd ed. Basingstoke, U.K.: Macmillan, 1994.

Bailey, Sydney Dawson. *How Wars End: The United Nations and the Termination of Armed Conflict, 1946–1964.* 2 vols. Oxford: Clarendon Press, 1982.

————. *The UN Security Council and Human Rights.* Basingstoke, U.K.: Macmillan; New York: St. Martin's Press, 1994.

Barros, James, ed. *The United Nations: Past, Present, and Future.* New York: Free Press, 1972.

Basu, R. *The United Nations: Structure and Functions of an International Organisation.* New Delhi: Sterling, 1993.

Bedjaoui, Mohammed. *The New World Order and the Security Council: Testing the Legality of Its Acts.* Dordrecht, Netherlands, and Boston, Mass.: M. Nijhoff, 1994.

Beigbeder, Yves. *The Internal Management of United Nations Organizations: The Long Quest for Reform.* New York: St. Martin's Press, 1996.

Bennett, Alvin Leroy. *International Organizations: Principles and Issues.* 6th ed. Englewood Cliffs, N.J.: Prentice Hall, 1995.

Bennys, Phyllis. *Calling the Shots: How Washington Dominates Today's UN.* New York: Olive Branch Press, 1996.

Bingham, June. *U Thant: The Search for Peace.* New York: Alfred A. Knopf, 1966.

Bishop, Peter V. "Canada and the Controversy Over the Financing of the United Nations Peacekeeping Operations." PhD dissertation. Toronto: University of Toronto, 1969.

Blodgett, Steven Alvah. "The Evolving Relationship Between the United Nations and International Non-Governmental Organizations: An Assessment of the Need for Institutional Reform." PhD dissertation. Kent, Ohio: Kent State University, 1982; Ann Arbor, Mich.: University Microfilms International, 1984.

Boudreau, Thomas Eugene. *Sheathing the Sword: The U.N. Secretary-General and the Prevention of International Conflict.* New York and Westport, Conn.: Greenwood Press, 1991.

Bourantonis, Dimitris, and Jarrod Weiner, eds. *The United Nations in the New World Order: The World Organization at Fifty.* New York: St. Martin's Press, 1995.

Boyd, Andrew. *Fifteen Men on a Powder Keg: A History of the UN Security Council.* London: Methuen, 1971.

Childers, Erskine B., ed. *Challenges to the United Nations: Building a Safer World.* London: Catholic Institute for International Relations, 1994.

Childers, Erskine B., and Brian Urquhart. *Renewing the United Nations System.* Special issue, *Development Dialogue* 1 (1994). Uppsala, Sweden: Dag Hammarskjöld Foundation, 1994.

Cleveland, Harlan. *Birth of a New World: An Open Moment for International Leadership.* Jossey-Bass Management Series. San Francisco, Calif.: Jossey-Bass Publishers, 1993.

Conetta, Karl, and Charles Knight. *Vital Force: A Proposal for the Overhaul of the UN Peace Operations System and for the Creation of a UN Legion.* Project on Defense Alternatives Research Monograph No. 4. Cambridge, Mass.: Commonwealth Institute, 1995.

Cox, Robert W., and Harold K. Jacobson. *The Anatomy of Influence: Decision-Making in International Organization.* New Haven, Conn.: Yale University Press, 1973.

Diehl, Paul Francis, ed. *The Politics of International Organizations: Patterns and Insights.* Chicago: Dorsey Press, 1989.

Donovan, Frank Robert. *Mr. Roosevelt's Four Freedoms: The Story Behind the United Nations Charter.* New York: Dodd, 1966.

Drakidis, Philippe. *The Atlantic and United Nations Charters: Common Law Prevailing for World Peace and Security.* Besançon, France: CRIPES, 1995.

Durch, William J., and Barry M. Blechman. *Keeping the Peace: The United Nations in the Emerging World Order.* Washington, D.C.: Henry L. Stimson Center, 1992.

Evans, Gareth. *Cooperating for Peace: The Global Agenda for the 1990s and Beyond.* St. Leonards, Australia: Allen & Unwin, 1993.

Falk, Richard A., Samuel S. Kim, and Saul H. Mendlowitz. *The United Nations and a Just World Order.* Boulder, Colo.: Westview Press, 1991.

Ferencz, Benjamin B. *New Legal Foundations for Global Survival: Security Through the Security Council.* Dobbs Ferry, N.Y.: Oceana Publications, 1994.

Fisas, Vivenç. *Blue Geopolitics: The United Nations Reform and the Future of the Blue Helmets.* London and New Haven, Conn.: Pluto Press, 1995.

Frye, William R., ed. *A United Nations Peace Force.* New York: Oceana, 1957.

Gaffen, Fred. *In the Eye of the Storm: A History of Canadian Peacekeeping.* Toronto: Deneau and Wayne, 1987.

Gavshon, Arthur L. *The Mysterious Death of Dag Hammarskjold.* New York: Walker, 1962.

Girardet, Edward R., ed. *Somalia, Rwanda, and Beyond: The Role of the International Media in Wars and Humanitarian Crisis.* Crosslines Special Report No. 1. Dublin: Crosslines Communications; New York: Italian Academy for Advanced Studies at Columbia University, 1995.

Granatstein, J.L., and David J. Bercuson. *War and Peacekeeping: From South Africa to the Gulf—Canada's Limited Wars.* Toronto: Key Porter Books, 1991.

Haas, Ernst B. *Why We Still Need the United Nations: Collective Management of International Conflict, 1945–1984.* Policy Paper in International Affairs No. 26. Berkeley, Calif.: Institute of International Studies, 1986.

Harderman, John W. *The United Nations and the Rule of Law: Charter Development Through the Handling of International Disputes and Situations.* Dobbs Ferry, N.Y.: Oceana, 1966.

Hill, Martin. *The United Nations System: Coordinating its Economic and Social Work.* Cambridge, U.K., and New York: Cambridge University Press, 1978.

Holtje, James. *Divided It Stands: Can the United Nations Work?* Atlanta, Ga.: Turner Publishing, 1995.

Lie, Trygve. *In the Cause of Peace: Seven Years With the United Nations.* New York: MacMillan, 1954.

Mays, Terry M. *Historical Dictionary of Multinational Peacekeeping.* Lanham, Md.: Scarecrow Press, 1996.

McCoubrey, H. *International Organizations and Civil Wars.* Aldershot, U.K., and Brookfield, Vt.: Dartmouth Press, 1995.

Mingst, Karen A., and Margaret P. Karns. *The United Nations in the Post–Cold War Era.* Boulder, Colo.: Westview Press, 1995.

Muller, Robert, and Douglas Roche. *Safe Passage into the Twenty-First Century: The United Nations Quest for Peace, Equality, Justice, and Development.* New York: Continuum, 1995.

Newcombe, Hanna. *Design for a Better World.* Lanham, Md.: University Press of America, 1983.

Organski, A. "The Veto as Viewed by the United States and the Soviet Union." PhD dissertation. New York: New York University, 1951.

Parsons, Anthony. *From Cold War to Hot Peace: UN Interventions, 1946–1994.* London: Penguin Books, 1995.

Patil, Anjali V. *The UN Veto in World Affairs, 1946–1990: A Complete Record and Case Histories of the Security Council's Veto.* Includes microfiche with the texts of resolutions and decisions adopted by the Security Council, 1946–1990. Sarasota, Fla.: UNIFO Publications, 1992.

Peterson, M.J. *The General Assembly in World Politics.* Boston: Allen & Unwin, 1986.

Rajan, Mannaraswamighala Sreeranga. *The Expanding Jurisdiction of the United Nations.* Bombay: N.M. Tripathi; Dobbs Ferry, N.Y.: Oceana, 1982.

Ramcharan, Bertrand G. *Keeping Faith With the United Nations.* Dordrecht, Netherlands, Boston, and Lancaster, U.K.: M. Nijhoff, 1987.

Righter, Rosemary. *Utopia Lost: The United Nations and World Order.* New York: Twentieth Century Fund, 1995.

Rivlin, Benjamin, and Leon Gordenker, eds. *The Challenging Role of the UN Secretary-General: Making "the Most Impossible Job in the World" Possible.* Westport, Conn.: Praeger, 1993.

Roberts, Adam. *Presiding Over a Divided World: Changing UN Roles, 1945–1993.* Occasional Paper Series, International Peace Academy. Boulder, Colo.: Lynne Rienner, 1994.

Rochester, Martin J. *Waiting for the Millennium: The United Nations and the Future World Order.* Columbia, S.C.: University of South Carolina Press, 1993.

Russett, Bruce. *Grasping the Democratic Peace: Principles for a Post–Cold War World.* Princeton, N.J.: Princeton University Press, 1993.

Saksena, Krishan Prasad. "The United Nations and Collective Security, 1945–1964: A Historical Analysis." PhD dissertation. New York: New York University, 1971.

Sen, Sudhir. *United Nations in Economic Development: Need for a New Strategy.* Dobbs Ferry, N.Y.: Oceana, 1969.

Sharp, Walter Rice. *The United Nations Economic and Social Council.* New York: Columbia University Press, 1969.

Simma, Bruno, ed. *Charter of the United Nations: A Commentary.* Oxford and New York: Oxford University Press, 1994.

Simons, Geoff. *The United Nations: A Chronology of Conflict.* New York: St. Martin's Press, 1994.

———. *UN Malaise: Power, Problems and Realpolitik.* Basingstoke, U.K.: Macmillan; New York: St. Martin's Press, 1995.

Stoessinger, John George. *The United Nations and the Superpowers: China, Russia and America.* 4th ed. New York: Random House, 1977.

———. *The Might of Nations: World Politics in Our Time.* 8th ed. New York: Random House, 1986.

Sutterlin, James S. *The United Nations and the Maintenance of International Security: A Challenge to be Met.* Westport, Conn.: Praeger, 1995.

Thant, U. *View from the UN: The Memoirs of U Thant.* New York: Doubleday, 1978.

Thorpe, Deryck. *Hammarskjold: Man of Peace.* Ilfracombe, U.K.: Stockwell, 1969.

Tomuschat, Christian, ed. *The United Nations at Age Fifty: A Legal Perspective.* The Hague and Boston: Kluwer Law International, 1995.

Waldheim, Kurt. *In the Eye of the Storm: A Memoir.* London: Weidenfeld & Nicolson, 1985.

Weiss, Thomas George. *The United Nations and Civil Wars.* Boulder, Colo.: Lynne Rienner, 1995.

Weiss, Thomas George, David P. Forsythe and Roger A. Coate. *The United Nations and Changing World Politics.* Boulder, Colo.: Westview Press, 1994.

Wellens, Karel C., ed. *Resolutions and Statements of the United Nations Security Council (1946–1992): A Thematic Guide.* 2nd ed. Dordrecht, Netherlands, and Boston: M. Nijhoff, 1993.

Whittaker, David J. *United Nations in Action.* Armonk, N.Y.: M.E. Sharpe, 1995.

Woodward, Susan L. *Balkan Tragedy: Chaos and Dissolution After the Cold War.* Washington, D.C.: Brookings Institution, 1995.

THE UNITED NATIONS SYSTEM
Principle Organs of the United Nations

INTERNATIONAL COURT OF JUSTICE

GENERAL ASSEMBLY

ECONOMIC AND SOCIAL COUNCIL

SECURITY COUNCIL

SECRETARIAT

TRUSTEESHIP COUNCIL

- Main and other sessional committees
- Standing committees and ad hoc bodies
- Other subsidiary organs and selected bodies

▶ UNRWA
United Nations Relief and Works Agency for Palestine Refugees in the Near East

▶ IAEA
International Atomic Energy Agency

▶ INSTRAW
International Research and Training Institute for the Advancement of Women

▶ ODCCP
United Nations Office for Drug Control and Crime Prevention

▶ OHCHR
Office of the United Nations High Commissioner for Human Rights

▶ UNCHS (Habitat)
United Nations Centre for Human Settlements

▶ UNCTAD
United Nations Conference on Trade and Development

▶ UNDP
United Nations Development Progamme

▶ UNIFEM
United Nations Development Fund for Women
▶ UNV
United Nations Volunteers

▶ UNEP
United Nations Environment Programme

▶ UNFPA
United Nations Population Fund

▶ UNHCR
Office of the United Nations High Commissioner for Refugees

▶ UNICEF
United Nations Children's Fund

▶ UNICRI
United Nations Interregional Crime and Justice Research Institute

▶ UNIDIR
United Nations Institute for Disarmament Research

▶ UNITAR
United Nations Institute for Training and Research

▶ UNOPS
United Nations Office for Project Services

▶ UNU
United Nations University

▶ WFP
World Food Programme

▶ ITC
International Trade Centre UNCTAD/WTO

- FUNCTIONAL COMMISSIONS
  Commission for Social Development
  ▶ United Nations Research Institute for Social Development (UNRISD)
  Commission on Crime Prevention and Criminal Justice
  Commission on Human Rights
  Commission on Narcotic Drugs
  Commission on Science and Technology for Development
  Commission on Sustainable Development
  Commission on the Status of Women
  Commission on Population and Development
  Statistical Commission

- REGIONAL COMMISSIONS
  Economic Commission for Africa (ECA)
  Economic Commission for Europe (ECE)
  Economic Commission for Latin America and the Caribbean (ECLAC)
  Economic and Social Commission for Asia and the Pacific (ESCAP)
  Economic and Social Commission for Western Asia (ESCWA)

- SESSIONAL AND STANDING COMMITTEES

- EXPERT, AD HOC AND RELATED BODIES

- Military Staff Committee
- Standing committees and ad hoc bodies
- International Criminal Tribunal for the former Yugoslavia
- International Criminal Tribunal for Rwanda

• UNSCOM
United Nations Special Commission (Iraq)

■ ILO
International Labour Organization

■ FAO
Food and Agriculture Organization of the United Nations

■ UNESCO
United Nations Educational, Scientific and Cultural Organization

■ WHO
World Health Organization

WORLD BANK GROUP

■ IBRD
International Bank for Reconstruction and Development

■ IDA
International Development Association

■ IFC
International Finance Corporation

■ MIGA
Multilateral Investment Guarantee Agency

■ IMF
International Monetary Fund

■ ICAO
International Civil Aviation Organization

■ UPU
Universal Postal Union

■ ITU
International Telecommunications Union

■ WMO
World Meteorological Organization

■ IMO
International Maritime Organization

■ WIPO
World Intellectual Property Organization

■ IFAD
International Fund for Agricultural Development

■ UNIDO
United Nations Industrial Development Organization

■ WTO*
World Trade Organization

OSG
Office of the Secretary-General

OIOS
Office of Internal Oversight Services

OLA
Office of Legal Affairs

DPA
Department of Political Affairs

DDA
Department for Disarmament Affairs

DPKO
Department of Peacekeeping Operations

OCHA
Office for the Co-ordination of Humanitarian Affairs

DESA
Department of Economic and Social Affairs

DGAACS
Department of General Assembly Affairs and Conference Services

DPI
Department of Public Information

DM
Department of Management

UNESCOORD
Office of the United Nations Security Co-ordinator

UNOG
UN Office at Geneva

UNOV
UN Office at Vienna

UNON
UN Office at Nairobi

▶ United Nations programmes and organs (representative)

■ Specialized agencies and other autonomous organizations within the UN system

• Other commissions, committees, and ad hoc and related bodies

* Not part of the United Nations system although has co-operating arrangements and practices with the UN